ADVANCED SPANISH ACADEMY COACHING

120 Technical, Tactical and Conditioning Practices from Top Spanish Coaches

Written by

David Aznar

Rafa Juanes

Manu Dorado

Fernando Gaspar

Published by

Advanced Spanish Academy Coaching

120 Technical, Tactical and Conditioning Practices from Top Spanish Coaches

First Published July 2014 by SoccerTutor.com

Info@soccertutor.com | www.SoccerTutor.com
UK: 0208 1234 007 | **US:** (305) 767 4443 | **ROTW:** +44 208 1234 007

ISBN 978-0-9576705-8-7

Copyright: SoccerTutor.com Limited © 2014. All Rights Reserved.

All rights reserved. No part of this publication may be reproduced, stored in a retrieval system, or transmitted in any form or by any means, electronic, mechanical, photocopy, recording or otherwise, without prior written permission of the copyright owner. Nor can it be circulated in any form of binding or cover other than that in which it is published and without similar condition including this condition being imposed on a subsequent purchaser.

Spanish to English Translation
Abby Parkhouse - abbyparkhouse@yahoo.co.uk

Edited by
Alex Fitzgerald - SoccerTutor.com

Cover Design by
Alex Macrides, Think Out Of The Box Ltd.
email: design@thinkootb.com Tel: +44 (0) 208 144 3550

Diagrams
Diagram designs by SoccerTutor.com. All the diagrams in this book have been created using SoccerTutor.com Tactics Manager Software available from www.SoccerTutor.com

Note: While every effort has been made to ensure the technical accuracy of the content of this book, neither the author nor publishers can accept any responsibility for any injury or loss sustained as a result of the use of this material.

CONTENTS

Practice Format	viii

CHAPTER 1: DAVID AZNAR — 1

Spanish Football Federation Youth Development Coach Profile	2
Technical / Tactical Training in Grassroots Football	3
Long Term Planning	4
Decision Making as a Key Factor	6
The Phases of Formative Training	9
The Importance of Learning	10
The Training Drills	12

Practices to Improve Vision & Spatial Awareness — 13

5 v 1 Passing and Possession Exercise	14
6 v 2 Possession Play with Switching Positions	15
6 v 3 Passing Square Possession Exercise	16
4 (+2) v 2 Support Play Possession Exercise	17
8 v 4 Passing Square Possession Exercise	18
4 Pairs Possession Game	19
3 Team Dynamic Vision Possession Game	20

Practices to Improve Possession — 21

10 v 5 Possession Play in a 2 Zone Transition Game	22
6 v 4 Fast Attacks in a Possession / Transition Game	23
Aerial Passing and Receiving 4 Zone Game	24
Passing and Receiving 4 Corners Possession Game	25
Vision, Awareness and Support Play in a 4 Corners Possession Game	26
Quick Finishing 4 Goals Possession Game	27
One-Two Combination Support Play in an 8 v 8 (+2) Possession Game	28
Possession Play with a 7 v 9 Numerical Disadvantage Transition Game	29
8 v 8 One-Two Combination Side Zone SSG	30
3 Team Support Play Possession Game	31
Quick One-Two End to End Possession Game	32
Passing through the Lines with Support Play in a 3 Team End to End Possession Game	33
4 Zone Dynamic Possession, Transition Play and Pressing Game	34
8 v 8 Support Play Possession Game	35

Practices to Improve Finishing — 36

4 v 4 Create Space and Finishing Small Sided Game	37
Quick Counter Attack with Wide Support Play in a 4 Goals Small Sided Game	38
Accurate Through Ball and Finishing in a 4 v 3 Attack	39
Continuous Crossing and Finishing Practice	40

CONTENTS

Passing in Behind and Finishing in a 4 v 3 Attack	41
Creating Space, Quick Combination Play and Finishing in a 6 v 6 Small Sided Game	42
Escaping a Marker in a 3 Zone Finishing Practice	43
Escaping a Marker and Finishing in a 4 v 4 (+2) Small Sided Game	44

CHAPTER 2: RAFA JUANES — 45

Villarreal CF Technical Academy Coordinator Profile — 46

Special Program Designed for Technical Improvement in Tactical Positioning	47
Characteristics of the Work	48
Actions on which to Work	49

Development of the Program: Centre Backs — 50

Tracking Back, Intercepting and Building up Play with a Long Diagonal Ball	52
Directing Headed Clearances from a Long Ball	53
Defensive Covering on the Flank and Challenging for the Ball	54
Defending Set Pieces with Opposed Man to Man Marking	55
Defending a High Long Ball with Headed Clearances	56

Special Program to Develop Technical Perfection through Tactical Positioning: Wide Players — 57

Playing Across the Back and a Full Back's Long Pass for Forward	59
Playing Across the Back and a Full Back's Long Diagonal Pass	60
Playing the Ball Along the Defensive Line to Switch the Point of Attack	61
Full Backs: Receive from the Goalkeeper, Short Dribble and Change of Direction	62
Technical Actions for Attacking on the Flank; 1 v 1 Play, Crossing and Finishing	63
Attacking on the Flank in 1 v 1 Situations with Switching Play	65
Specific Back 4 Defensive Movements when the Ball is Out Wide	66
Tracking Back, Intercepting the Ball and Controlled Defensive Clearances	68

Special Program to Develop Technical Perfection through Tactical Positioning: Centre Midfielders — 69

Coordinated Movements of the Centre Midfielders when Building up Play from the Back	71
Switching Play from One Flank to the Other using the Centre Midfielders	75
Controlled Interception from a Goal Kick and Change of Direction to Start an Attack	76
Modifying Positioning while Running Backwards & Controlled Headed Clearances to Start an Attack	77
Centre Midfield Combination Play after Defending a Long Ball	78
Special Program to Develop Technical Perfection Through Tactical Positioning: Forwards	80
Collective and Coordinated Movements of the Front 6 With & Without the Ball	82
Coordinated Movements for Attacking on the Flanks with Crossing & Finishing	84
Movement of the Forwards: Diagonal Runs to Escape a Marker	86

CONTENTS

Forward Play: Receiving with Back to Goal, Protecting the Ball and Finishing	87
Technical: Shooting on the Run from a Tight Angle	88
Diagonal Run, Quick Change of Direction and Finishing using Both Feet	89
Diagonal Run Across the Penalty Area and Finishing Against the Direction of the Run	90
Diagonal Run Across the Penalty Area, Receive with Back to Goal, Turn and Shoot	91

CHAPTER 3: MANU DORADO — 92

Real Madrid Academy Coach Profile	93
Concepts for Training: Learning to Deal with Specific Situations	94
Why is it Important to Learn Through Concepts?	95
Concepts of the Game	97
Specific Learning Concepts as a Tool for Creating Intelligent Players	102
Collective Movement to Defend the Area in a 6 v 4 Situation	104
Methodology Based on Guided Discovery Through Questions	105
Practice 1: Building Up Play and Decision Making in a 5 v 4 Attack	108
Practice 2: Decision Making on the Flank in a 2 v 2 Small Sided Game	111
Practice 3: Correct Distances, Positioning & Movement of the Defensive Line	112
Practice 4: Attacking Flank Play in a 3 v 3 Small Sided Game	113

CHAPTER 4: FERNANDO GASPAR — 114

Fitness Specialist Coach Profile	115
Introduction: Physical Preparation for Ages 14-18	116

Practices to Improve Conditioning: Stamina, Strength & Speed — 120

Dynamic 'Futbol' Conditioning Circuit Training	121
Continuous 1 v 1 Duels and Finishing Practice	122
Man to Man Marking 7 v 7 Small Sided Game	123
Timing Forward Runs and Finishing Practice	124
Global 'Futbol' Specific Circuit Training	125
Circuit Training with Combination Play & Finishing	126
Strength, Power and Finishing Practice	127

Practices to Improve Speed, Agility Coordination & Strength — 128

Coordinated Runs and Movement with Crossing & Finishing	129
One-Two Combination, Dribbling and Finishing in a Coordination & Speed Exercise	130
Attacking Combination Play on the Flank in a Speed and Acceleration Practice	131
Speed and Agility in a 1 v 1 Duel with Finishing	132
Quick Reactions & Finishing in a 3 v 3 Practice	133
Possession Play & 3 v 2 Fast Break Attacks	134
Acceleration and Finishing in 1 v 1 Duels	135
Acceleration and Attacking Flank Play 2 v 2 Duel	136
Technical: Receiving and Finishing Under Pressure in the Penalty Area	137

CONTENTS

Attacking at Speed and Finishing from Different Angles in 1 v 1 Duels	138
Coordination and Speed of Footwork Exercise	139
Quick Reactions and Finishing Speed Circuit	140
Speed, Agility, Awareness and Decision Making Pattern of Play	141
Technical: Ball Control and Passing in a Continuous Circuit	142
Speed and Agility Practice with Accurate Passing	143
Playing Under Physical Pressure in a 4 v 4 (+5) Possession Game	144
Coordination, Agility and Finishing Speed Race	145
Technical: Escaping the Marker in a Continuous Finishing Practice	146
Jumping Power, Ball Control and Finishing Practice	147
Explosive Power, Coordination and Heading Practice	148
Speed and Coordination Exercise	149
Possession and Speed of Play in a 3 v 3 Small Sided Game with Cone Gates	150
Acceleration and Explosive Power with Physical Resistance	151
Ball Control and Dribbling Exercise in Channels	152
Running with the Ball and Changing Speed	153
Agility and Support Play in a One Touch Passing Combination Practice	154
Changing Direction at Speed and Shooting Practice	155
Power and Speed in a 3 v 3 Small Sided Game	156
Agility, Speed, Strength and Fast 3 v 3 Attack in a Continuous Circuit	157
Changing Pace and Direction with Quick Feet in a Speed Exercise with One-Two Combination	158
Support Angles in a 4 v 1 Possession Exercise	159

Strength & Conditioning Circuit Games — **160**

Technical, Speed and Conditioning Training in a Continuous Circuit	161
Conditioning Exercise With and Without the Ball: One-Two Combination Running Circuit	162
Tactical Shape with Position Specific Passing and Conditioning Exercise	163
Conditioning Circuit: 6 v 6 Practice Game and Interval Training	164
Technical Passing, Combination Play and Conditioning Practice	165
Agility, Coordination and Speed Interval Training	166
Interval Training with Technical Work in a 5 Zone Circuit	167
Conditioning with Position Specific Team Shape Exercise	168
Endurance 8 v 8 Small Sided Game with Dribbling End Zones + Sprinting Exercise	169
Goalkeeper Support Play and Conditioning in a 3 Zone Continuous Possession Game	170
Explosive Power 6 v 6 Fast Support Play Dynamic Small Sided Game	171
Aerobic Power 8 v 8 Small Sided Game	172

PRACTICE FORMAT

There are 4 different Spanish coaches each with a range of practices.

Each practice includes clear diagrams with supporting training notes such as:

• Name of Practice
• Objective of Practice
• Description of Practice
• Variation or Progression (if applicable)
• Coaching Points

KEY

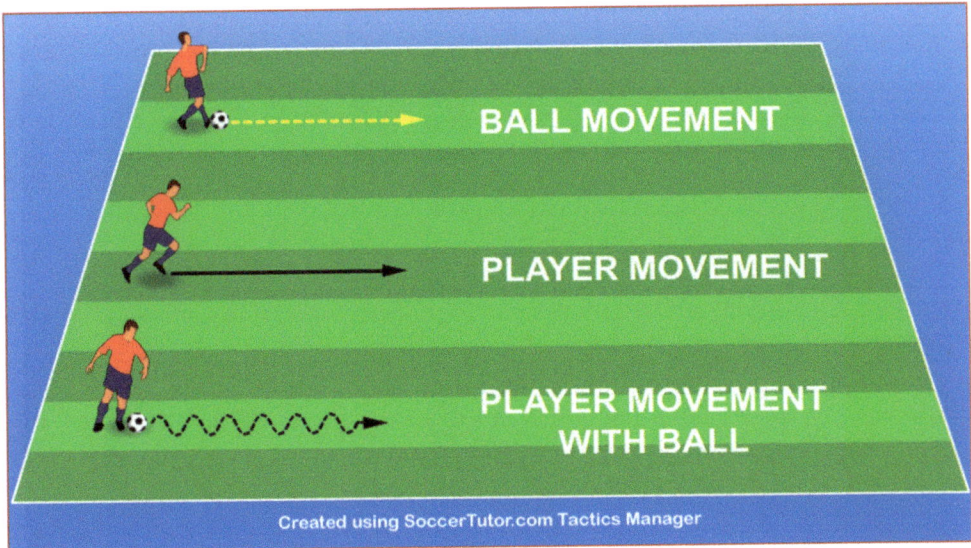

CHAPTER 1

DAVID AZNAR

Spanish Football Federation Youth Development Coach

Former Atlético Madrid & Real Madrid Academy Coach

SPANISH FOOTBALL FEDERATION YOUTH DEVELOPMENT COACH PROFILE

David Aznar
Spanish Football Federation Youth Development Coach

Previous Coaching positions:
- Atlético Madrid U18 academy
- Real Madrid academy coach

Credentials:
- UEFA A Licence
- Bachelor of Physical Education
- Selección Española de Fútbol RFEF (Spanish National team)

TECHNICAL / TACTICAL TRAINING IN GRASSROOTS FOOTBALL

Football is a game. As such, the best way to learn is through practice. As it is a game, it should also be fun and recreational. The purpose of the game lies in providing the collective with all of the individual skills necessary to overcome the opposition during competition.

Grassroots football, by its very name, is the name given to the formative years of football training before the players embark on the road to acquiring the different physical and technical skills, as well as the competitive and strategic tactics and the social and psychological aspects of football.

The main objective of grassroots football should be to mould people through football, that know how to play in any category, respecting the rules, sporting values, their opponents, their environment, the referees, the game itself and above all, enjoying the practice more than the result, and to never stop doing so.

Grassroots football always triggers debate within the football world. The work done at the youth academies of the big clubs is often criticised because the players do not go on to play for the first team.

Apart from the opportunities given to young players in the academies, conflicts may arise in the lack of continuity and progression from the basic work.

There may be poor judgement in regards to an individual's progression. The young player may not be able to adapt or have the capacity to learn and stages may be skipped in the evolution or individual progression of the youngster.

David Aznar Spanish Football Federation Youth Development Coach

LONG TERM PLANNING

To plan is to draw a map that allows us to organise the journey without deviating from the most important objective, "the training of the youngster".

We have to adopt a method that ensures the development of high performance motor skills, guaranteed through effective teaching and motivation.

Planning is to anticipate (visualise) the future, using past experiences and the potential available in the present.

Long Term Planning for Player's Development

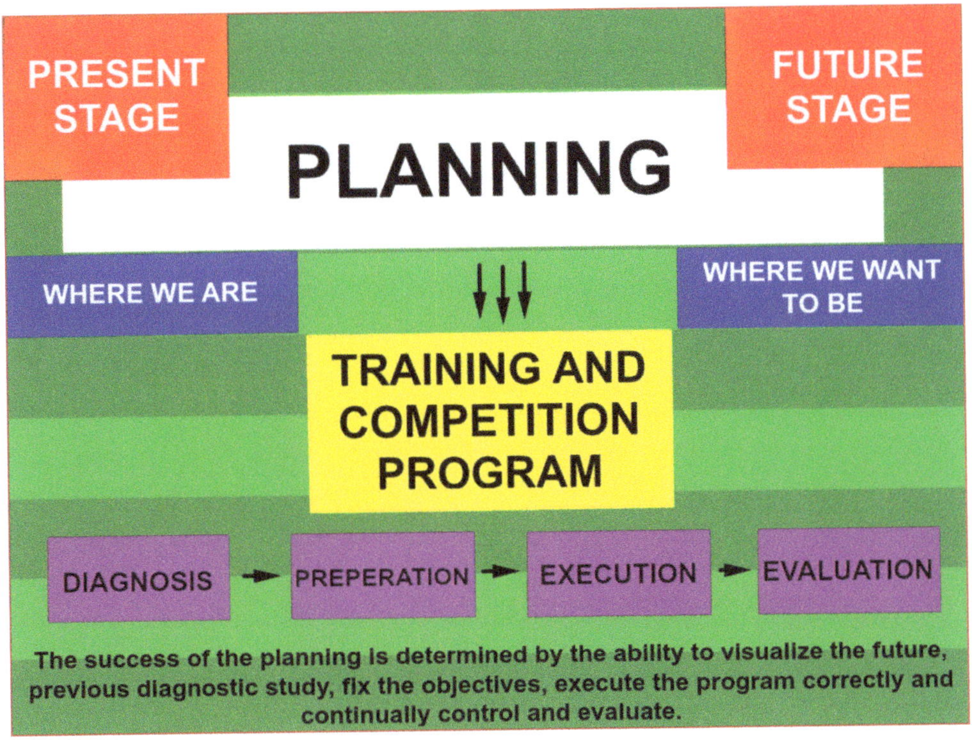

![Planning diagram: PRESENT STAGE (WHERE WE ARE) → PLANNING → FUTURE STAGE (WHERE WE WANT TO BE). TRAINING AND COMPETITION PROGRAM: DIAGNOSIS → PREPERATION → EXECUTION → EVALUATION. The success of the planning is determined by the ability to visualize the future, previous diagnostic study, fix the objectives, execute the program correctly and continually control and evaluate.]

"Only training performed over a number of years allows you to obtain a high level of sporting performance. Its structure should be developed considering a multitude of factors".
Platonov (1998)

The key factors that define good planning are:

- Consistency between the desired goal and reality.
- Respect the individuality of the child.
- Defined plans for each stage of development.
- Avoid obsession with immediate performance.
- Increase the number of sessions and hours every year.
- Increase the number and intensity of competition.
- Gradually increase the training load (volume and intensity).

To be successful each stage must be adapted in the best possible way.

The ultimate performance of any athlete will depend not only on their natural instincts, but on the correct management and training methods in each of these phases.

General Goals:

- Improve their playing capabilities.
- Adapt the football to suit each child's capabilities and characteristics.
- Encourage the child's growth.
- Educate the child in healthy habits through football.
- Improve the technique combined with tactics.

The differences that should define each stage of football during the early years should be adapted to the characteristics and capabilities that the player manifests depending on their age or level, considering the goals and different ways of working appropriate to each.

A child is not a senior in miniature. This is why I am against applying methods and some forms of high performance training drills with juniors.

David Aznar Spanish Football Federation Youth Development Coach

DECISION MAKING AS A KEY FACTOR

"Without the intelligence to play, the (technical) ability becomes an aimless virtue".
J. Valdano

When you consider that in more than 50% of cases, loss of possession results from poor decision making and not from a technical deficiency, you see that these problems deserve more attention from us.

Having given priority to technique and the strict compliance with the coach's instructions without sufficiently including the player in the problem solving process, the young players development in the basic aspects of the game have been impeded.

That is the only reason why today we do not have enough intelligent players capable of solving multiple problems as they occur during a game.

TECHNIQUE and **TACTICS** are inseparable and it makes no sense to separate the "do" with the "how" and "when" and, above all, the "what" and "why" we do it. It is important for the success of any team to know not only how to pass the ball, but to know when, where and why the ball is being passed using one technique or another.

"Football is the simplest game that exists. The entire world knows it; the difficult thing is to play it".
J. Cruyff

Intelligence in footballers leads them on a search for the solutions to each problem that arises during competition.

Each position on the pitch needs a different type of intelligence; that of a goalkeeper is different to that of a central defender or an attacker.

You cannot solve defensive problems in the same way you solve those that arise during the attacking phase or in the goalmouth.

The reality is that the majority of coaches choose to ignore the importance of developing each individual player's intelligence in the footballer's teaching-learning process.

This is not because they do not appreciate it, but because they do not know how to utilise a less rigid and authoritarian style of coaching in which the player is the protagonist (a thinking footballer) and not one solely executing orders.

David Aznar Spanish Football Federation Youth Development Coach

Trainers and coaches should be aware that the development of game intelligence in football primarily involves teaching your players:

- To know how to perceive and understand a game situation through prior knowledge and experience.

- To be able to confront this situation with other similar situations in order to make the correct decision that mentally resolves the inherent problem.

- Know how to execute the previously thought out action without delay.

The ability to anticipate, which always precedes the optimal perception and decision making, is an important weapon in the armoury of an intelligent player.

Player Intelligence: Process of Decision Making

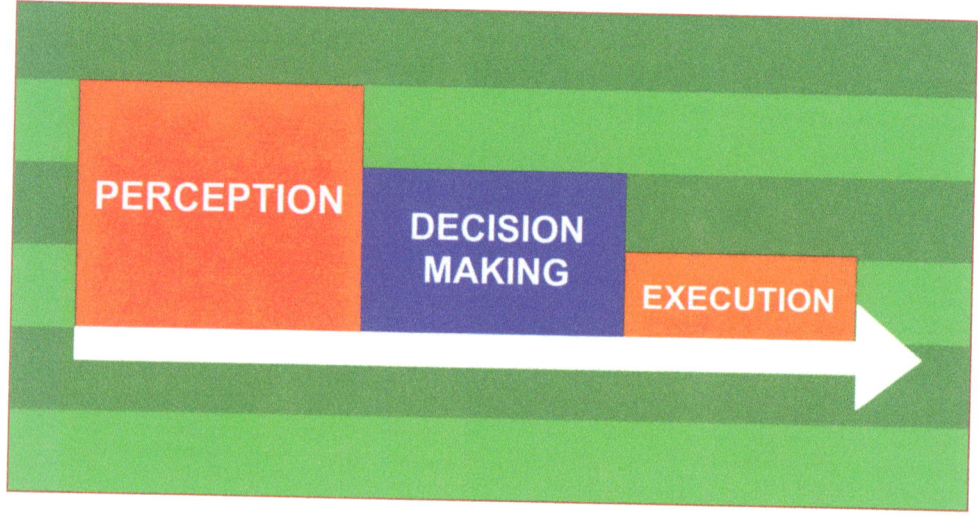

Important Repetitive Questions for the Coach

"The talented coaches are those who let the players discover the game, informing them of the basics, that teaches them to think and decide and encourages them to play, to take risks enthusiastically and unapologetically and allows them to enjoy the game as that is the best way to make them efficient…."

Angel Cappa

"The training drills should be faithful and develop a cognitive processing similar to that found during competition".

Important Processes for Full Player Development

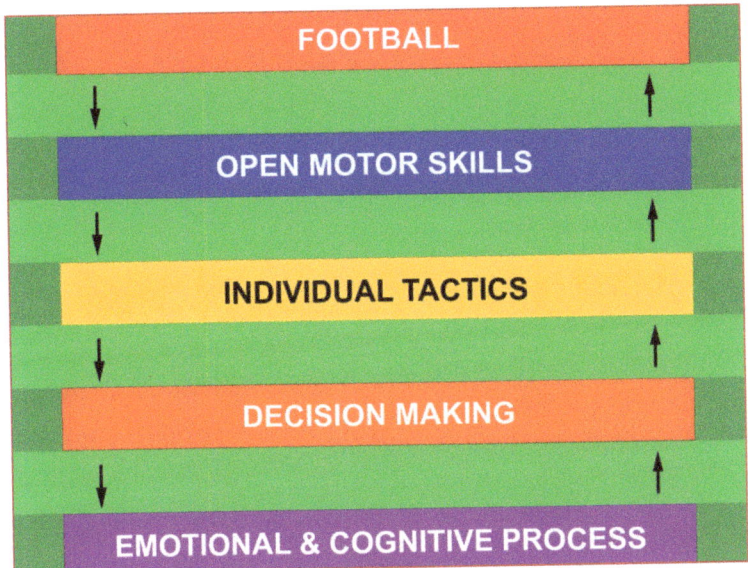

David Aznar Spanish Football Federation Youth Development Coach

THE PHASES OF FORMATIVE TRAINING

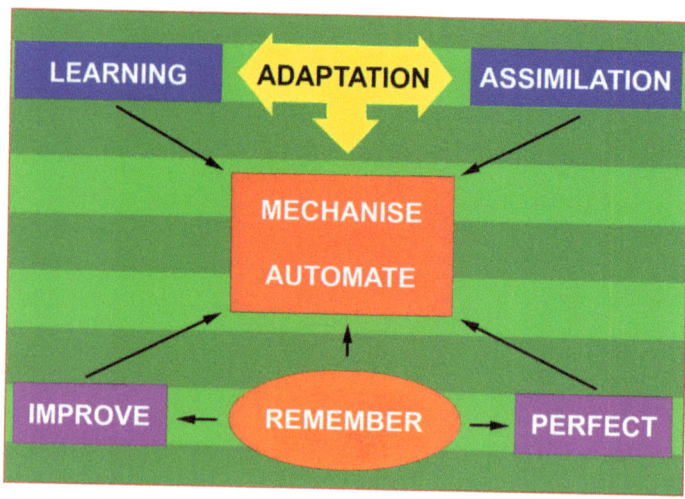

To achieve the best technical and tactical performance, the player should go through an organised, evolutionary and progressive learning process.

This process is divided into different phases that we use at the right time to plan determined objectives.

1. Learning: Acquire the basic knowledge in order to execute and make decisions, fixing technical movements into memory behaviour.

2. Adaptation: Acquire the skills necessary to accommodate mental and physical techniques and tactics to different game situations and circumstances.

3. Assimilation: Understand what has been learnt in order to execute it correctly. Incorporate prior knowledge, giving them a sense of understanding and allowing them to implement it.

4. Mechanise: Provide a regularity to the actions and decision making, so that it becomes a a mechanical process.

5. Automate: Make the most elementary physical or mental processes for decision making (automatic or involuntary).

6. Remember: Bring situations and past experiences to memory and have them present in current situations and subsequent actions.

7. Improve: Increase the capacity for analysis, resolution and implementation in different game situations.

8. Perfect: Give the best motor solution to the best cognitive solution with the highest degree of quality and detail.

David Aznar Spanish Football Federation Youth Development Coach

THE IMPORTANCE OF LEARNING

Why?

'Football is a game of a tactical nature, therefore it must be taught from that perspective.'
O. Cano

'Never run for the sake of it, there is always something that causes the certain behaviour of the player and that something is associated with an understanding of the game.'
Sanz, 2001

'Football requires mental ability rather than just the ability to play.'
Dewey, 1951

'Knowing means understanding.'
V. Glasesfeld, 1991

What for?

'To adapt to the different circumstances dictated by each action.'
Lillo, 2000

'The player will face high levels of uncertainty.'
Mombaerts, 2000

'Create players with the capacity to play with knowledge and not simply play.'
O. Cano

'The player will look for a reason to do things and although the execution may be poor, do not fault the intention.'
Lillo, 2000

How?

'Getting the player to learn the concepts and find solutions without telling them in a direct way but through games, activities and training drills.'
Lillo, 2000

'Preparing exercises based on real game situations that allow open solutions.'
Sainz, 2002

'Encourage the players to think and act constantly, drawing on motivators and involving them in problem solving situations that mirror real game situations.'
Garganta, 1997

David Aznar Spanish Football Federation Youth Development Coach

The Importance of Learning: Understanding the Player's Needs

There is no teaching without learning but unfortunately there is a lot of learning without teaching.

Objectives of our sessions:

To analyse and diagnose different situations, the demands of the tasks set out and the player's own situation (developing personal action strategies).

1. Encourage deviation from the "norm".
2. Tolerate uncertainty and respect the right of the players to make an error.
3. Offer opportunities for the players to discover avoiding direct teaching.
4. Increase the feeling of competence and confidence in their own resources as athletes.

Process of Learning Cycle

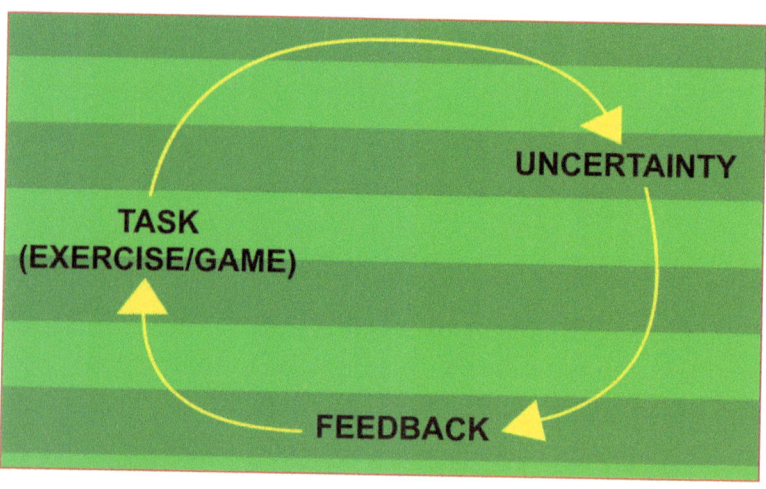

David Aznar Spanish Football Federation Youth Development Coach

THE TRAINING DRILLS

The most important thing with training is to train. The task is the main focus of the training so that the player actively participates in their learning.

This classification for the practical design of the drills, simple while at the same time complex, homogenous while varied, is based on the principals and fundamental aspects of training; warm up, primary objective and cool down.

Within the training there are games, analytical exercises (always incorporating decision making) and group analytical tasks based on specific and general play.

These are based on both attacking and defensive principals, both individual and collective play and competitive situations, all of which are indispensable in the development of a player's learning of the game.

Everything described can be adapted to any age, team, class or club because they are elementary exercises and tasks, each of which are progressive and may be adapted, improved and complicated using all of the variables that we can handle:

Space, number of participants, open or closed decision making and specific positioning.

All of the tasks are designed at their most basic so that we may add concepts, problems, variants and rules according to the group, team, category and individuals.

The idea behind the underlying methodology is to get each player to master the task and to know why they are doing so. This saves time making the training more economical.

If the player understands the methodology, the sessions will be more dynamic.

The coach serves up the ingredients that form the basis of the exercise.

The proposed training methods revolve around situation play, are dynamic and require group participation. Decision making and football responsibilities are constant.

What follows are a number of readily applicable training exercises using the cognitive and comprehensive methodology that we have learnt about over the previous pages.

Practices to Improve Vision & Spatial Awareness

David Aznar Spanish Football Federation Youth Development Coach

5 v 1 Passing and Possession Exercise

10 min

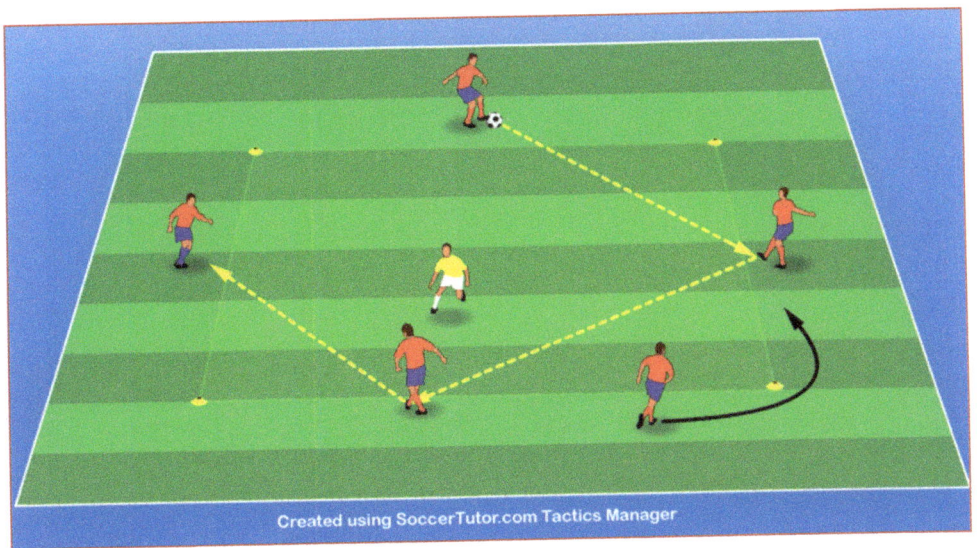

Objective
To develop passing, awareness of space, maintaining possession and player movement.

Description
In a 6 x 6 yard square, we have 5 players outside the area (2 on one side and 1 on each of the other sides) and 1 player inside (yellow shirt).

The outer players try to keep possession of the ball and the player in the centre tries to intercept it.

When a player on the side where there are 2 players passes the ball, their teammate must run to a side where there is only 1 player.

When a player loses the ball, that same player swaps roles with the inside player.

Variation
Play the ball in the air.

Coaching Points
1. Body shape should be open and players should use the back foot to receive/pass.
2. Improve the speed of play by limiting the players to 1 touch.

David Aznar Spanish Football Federation Youth Development Coach

6 v 2 Possession Play with Switching Positions

10 min

Objective
To develop passing, awareness of space and maintaining possession with switching positions.

Description
In an area 10 x 20 yards, we have 6 players along the outside of the area (1 in each corner and 2 in the middle by the red cones). There are 2 players inside. The outer players try to keep possession of the ball while the inside players try and intercept it.

The 4 corner players are limited to 2 touches and the middle players (by the red cones) are limited to 1 touch.

Each time the outer players (in the corners) pass the ball, they change positions with the players in the middle. In order for the inside players to stop defending, they must touch the ball (either 1 or both depending on the level of difficulty you require).

Coaching Points
1. Make sure the players communicate (verbal/optical) with their teammates, especially when switching positions.
2. The emphasis should be on the accuracy of the passes as players are positioned in specific areas (in the corners or on the red cones).
3. The 2 inside players need to work together to apply pressure and block the passing lanes.

David Aznar Spanish Football Federation Youth Development Coach

6 v 3 Passing Square Possession Exercise

10 min

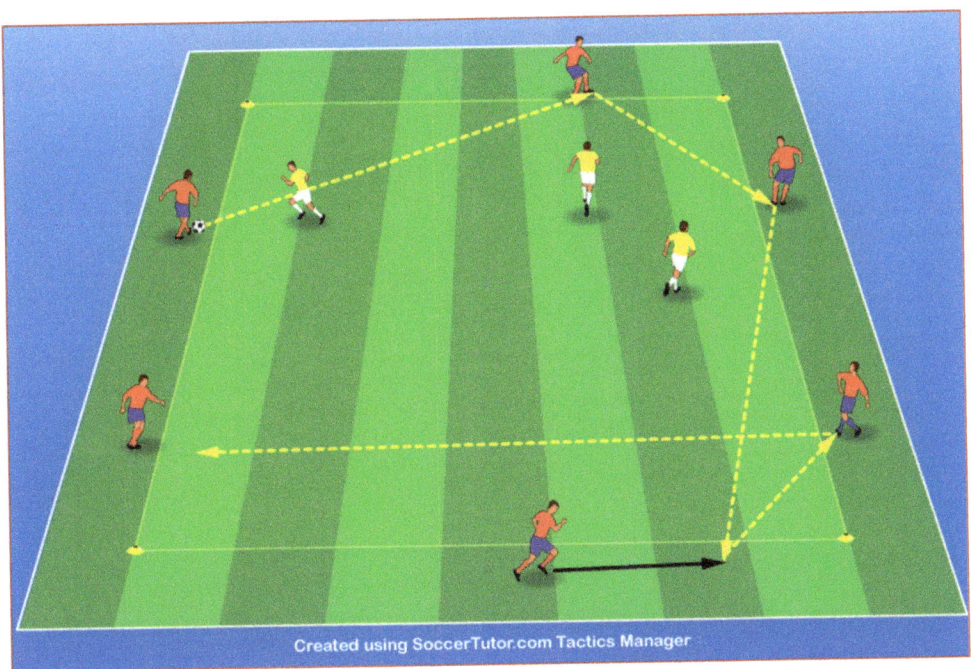

Objective
To develop passing, awareness of space, maintaining possession and player movement.

Description
In a 15 yard square, there are 6 players outside (positioned as shown) and 3 players inside.

The players around the outside try to keep possession of the ball while the players inside try to win/intercept it.

The outside players are limited to 2 touches. To make it more difficult you can indicate to the players where they must play the ball or make the inside players touch the ball 3 times before they are allowed to stop defending.

Change the players roles 1 at a time or in threes.

Variation
Limit all players to 1 touch.

David Aznar Spanish Football Federation Youth Development Coach

4 (+2) v 2 Support Play Possession Exercise   *15 min*

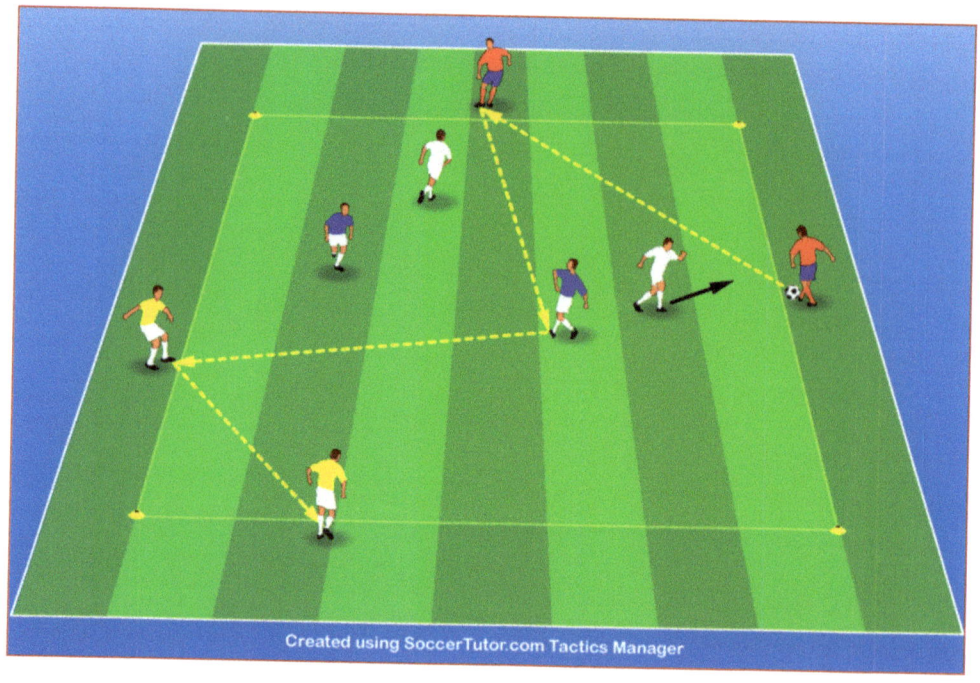

Objective
To develop passing, awareness of space, movement and good support play.

Description
In an 8 yard square, we have 4 players around the outside (1 on each side). Inside we have 2 centre midfielders (blue - holding players) with 2 defensive markers (white).

All the players are in pairs. The players in possession are limited to 3 touches.

If the markers touch the ball, the pair that lose the ball move to the marking role. Those that steal it move to the holding role and those already in that role move to the outside.

Coaching Points
1. The holding players need to use the correct angles/distances for their support play.
2. The correct body shape should be monitored (opening up) and receiving the ball with the back foot (foot furthest away from the ball).

David Aznar Spanish Football Federation Youth Development Coach

8 v 4 Passing Square Possession Exercise

12 min

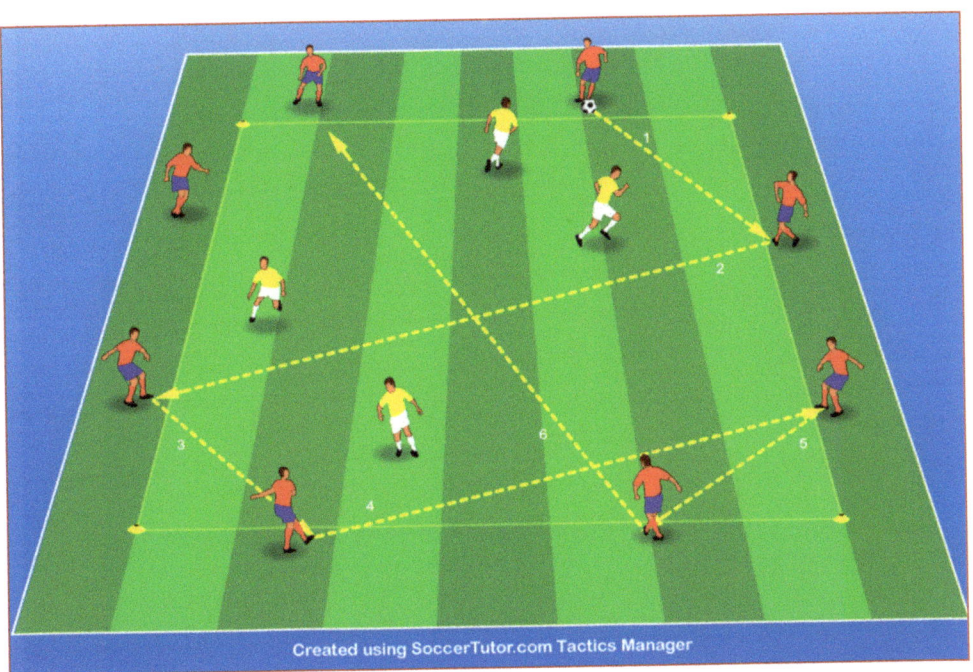

Objective
To develop passing, awareness of space, maintaining possession and player movement.

Description
In a 20 yard square, we play an 8v4 possession game. There are 2 players on each side of the square with 4 defensive players inside. The players around the outside try to keep possession of the ball while the inside players try to steal it. Limit the players to 2 touches.

The outside players are not allowed to pass to the player on the same side of the square. In order for the inside players to stop defending, they must touch the ball (1, 2 or 3 of them depending on the difficulty).

When changing the player roles, you can do so individually, in pairs or in groups of 4.

Coaching Points
1. Body shape should be open and players should use the back foot to receive/pass.
2. Improve the speed of play by limiting the players to 1 touch.

David Aznar Spanish Football Federation Youth Development Coach

4 Pairs Possession Game   15 min

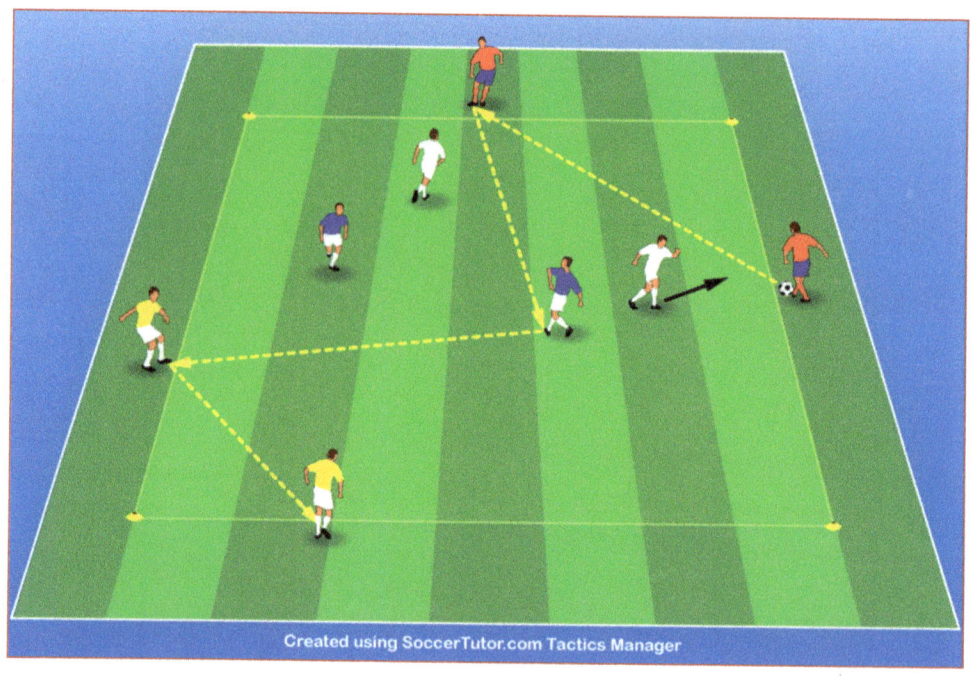

Objective
To develop passing, awareness and player movement within a competitive possession game.

Description
In a 10 yard square, we have 4 teams of 2. There are 2 teams outside and the other 2 are inside. 1 team keeps possession with the outside pairs and the other team (white) try to win the ball.

The outside players are limited to 1 touch and the inside players play with 2 touches.

The coach counts how many times each team wins the ball from each of the other 3 teams within a time period. We can also time how long it takes for each team to steal the ball a certain number of times.

Coaching Points
1. This is a competition so insist on a high speed of play and intensity.
2. The inside players should check away from their marker before moving to receive.

3 Team Dynamic Vision Possession Game

10 min

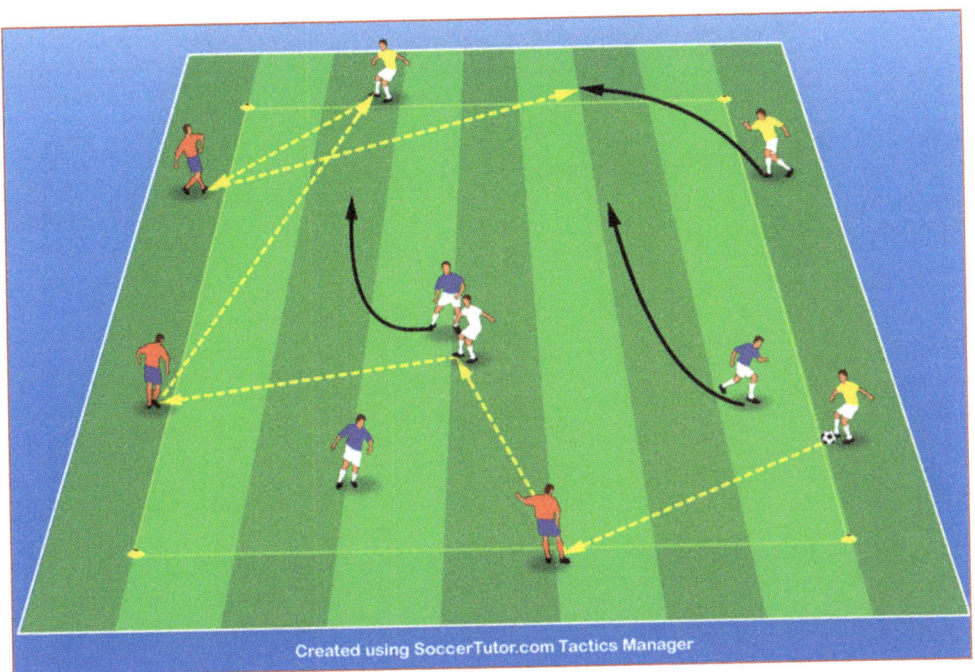

Objective
To develop vision and awareness with passing, possession and player movement.

Description
In an area 10 x 20 yards, there are 6 players around the outside in 2 teams of 3 (2 players on each of the longer sides and 1 on each of the shorter sides). There is a holding midfielder inside (white) and 3 defending players inside (blue).

The players around the outside try to keep possession with the support of the holding midfielder, while the blue players try to win/intercept the ball.

When a player on one of the sides where there are 2 players plays a pass, 1 of those players must then move to a side where there is only 1 player.

If a blue players wins the ball, they swap positions with the player that lost the ball. Change the player in the holding position every so often so that each player has a turn in that position.

David Aznar Spanish Football Federation Youth Development Coach

Practices to Improve Possession

David Aznar Spanish Football Federation Youth Development Coach

10 v 5 Possession Play in a 2 Zone Transition Game   **15 min**

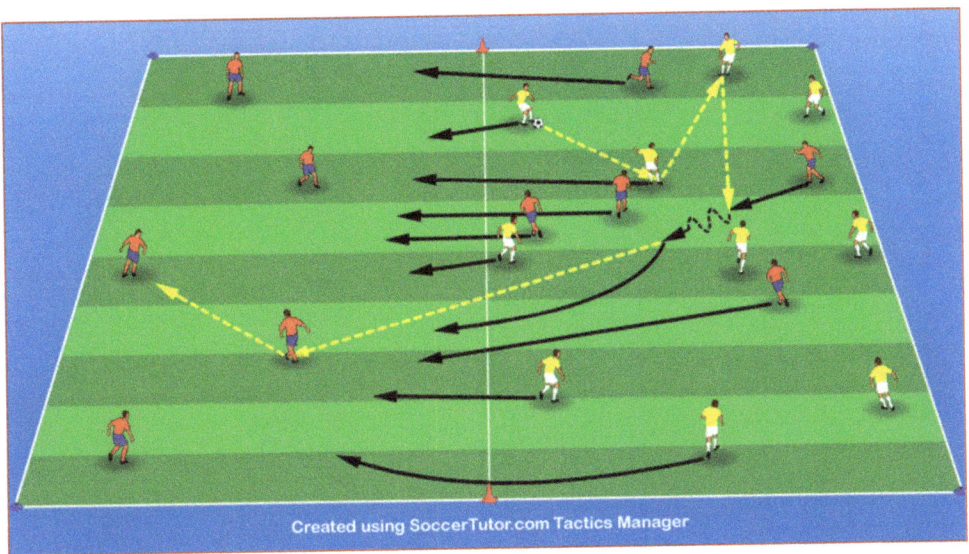

Objective
To develop team possession and quick transition play (attack/defence).

Description
In an area 40 x 40 yards, we play with 2 teams of 10 players. One team is split between the 2 zones. 5 players try to win the ball from 10 opposition players in one zone, while the other 5 players wait in the other zone.

The team with 10 players try to keep possession and are limited to 2 touches. When the defending team win the ball, they must pass to their teammates in the other zone (using unlimited touches) and then all players move to that area to try to keep possession of the ball.

They are not allowed to move until one of their 5 teammates has touched the ball. 5 of the opposing team then also move across to the opposite zone to try and win the ball back.

Coaching Points
1. The 5 defending players need to press collectively to win the ball (one closing down the ball carrier with the others marking or preventing the possible passes being made).
2. When possession is won, the players need to react quickly to run across to the other zone and provide support for their teammates to maintain possession.

David Aznar Spanish Football Federation Youth Development Coach

6 v 4 Fast Attacks in a Possession / Transition Game   15 min

Objective
We work on passing, possession/transition play and fast attacks in 6v4 situations.

Description
In an area 40 x 40 yards in the centre of the pitch, we play 6v6 inside the zone.

Once a team completes 6 passes (supported by their 4 teammates outside), the 6 inside players can attack the opposition at the other end. The 4 supporting players from the opposing team defend. This creates a 6v4 situation for the attack.

When they have scored or when the attack ends, the opposition's goalkeeper quickly plays the ball into the central zone to a teammate and they have the same aim in the opposite direction. The 6 attacking players must retreat very quickly (transition from attack to defence).

Coaching Points
1. For the attack, players should look to pass in behind the defensive line and make runs into the penalty area - the 4 outside defenders are not allowed in the penalty area.
2. Teams need to react quickly and regroup for the transition from attack to defence.

David Aznar Spanish Football Federation Youth Development Coach

Aerial Passing and Receiving 4 Zone Game

20 min

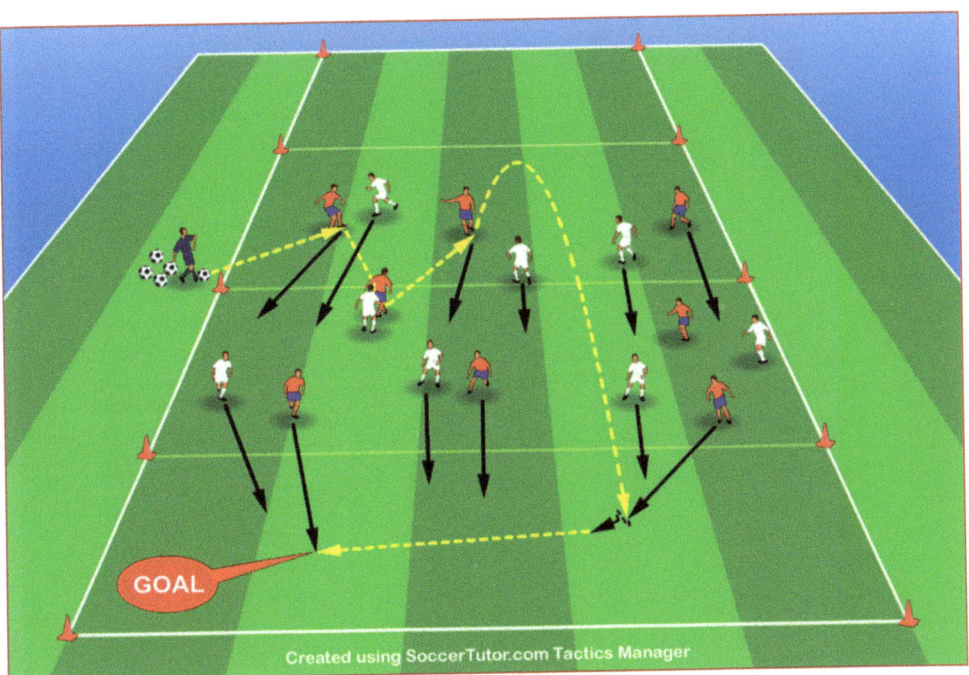

Objective
To develop aerial passing, running in behind and good control of the ball (first touch).

Description
In an area 70 x 70 yards, we divide the pitch into 4 zones. The central zones are 20 x 40 yards and the outside zones are 15 x 40 yards. Each team has 8 players.

One team has possession and all the players must be inside 2 zones. The objective is to pass the ball in the air over one zone (as shown in the diagram from zone 3 to zone 1) to a teammate who makes a run into an empty zone. The player must control the ball before it touches the ground and pass immediately within that zone; this counts as a goal.

The rest of the players move across so every player is within 2 zones again and the practice continues. In this example (diagram) the reds would now aim to play an aerial pass into zone 3.

Coaching Points
1. The accuracy, height and weight of the aerial pass is key, so the player is able to control it within the empty zone.
2. The player controlling the pass should do so with the part of the body which is required (head, chest, thigh, foot).

Passing and Receiving 4 Corners Possession Game 20 min

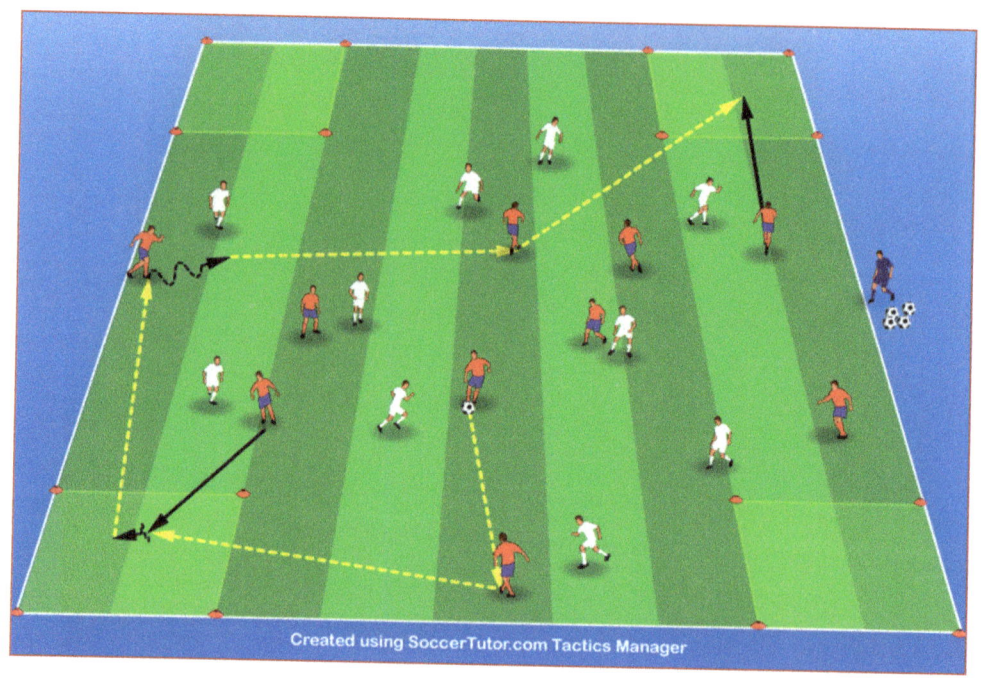

Objective
To develop possession play and passing/receiving in tight areas.

Description
Using half a full sized pitch, we have 10 x 10 yard squares marked out in each of the 4 corners.

We play a 10v10 game and all players are limited to 2 touches. In order to score a goal, the teams must receive a pass inside each of the 4 corner boxes whilst on the move.

Players are not allowed to be static inside one of the zones waiting for the pass, nor can the corner zones be defended from within. However, the team in possession can play in the zones they have already received in to retain possession.

Coaching Points
1. Players need to be constantly moving to create space and maintain possession.
2. To create space, players need to check away from their markers before moving to receive.
3. The passes into the corner zones need to be with the correct weight and timed for the run.

David Aznar Spanish Football Federation Youth Development Coach

Vision, Awareness and Support Play in a 4 Corners Possession Game

20 min

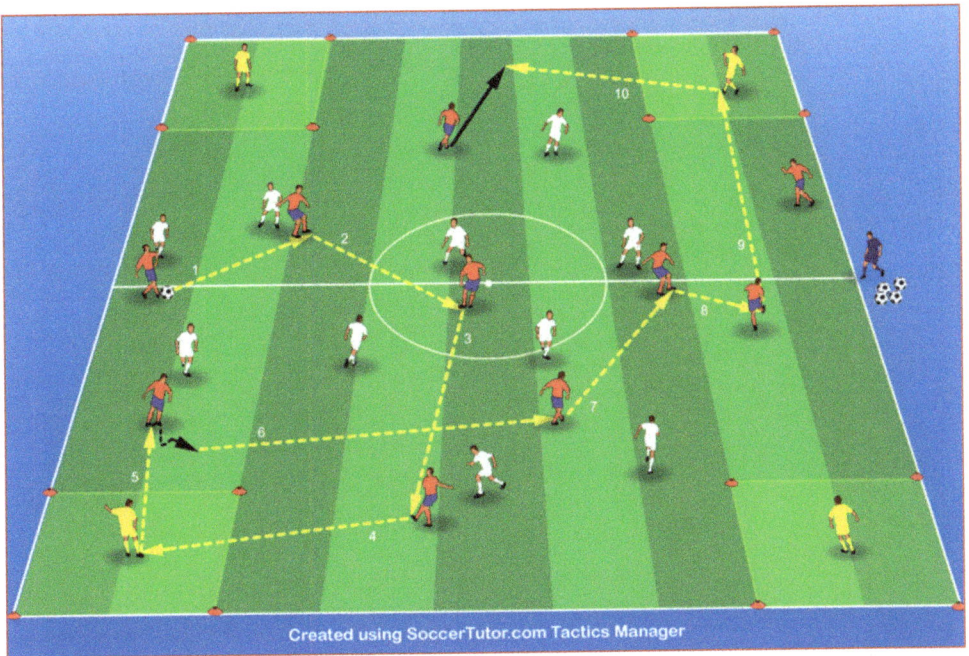

Objective
To develop possession play; vision, awareness, decision making, support movements and passing/receiving.

Description
We use the area in between both penalty areas and play 10v10 game again with 4 extra neutral players in the 10 x 10 yard corner zones. Players are limited to 3 touches and the neutral players have 1 touch.

There are 4 corner zones with a neutral player in each one. To score a point, a team must play the ball to one of the neutral players who must pass it back successfully to a member of the same team. The team attempts to repeat the same action in each of the 4 corners.

Coaching Points
1. Players need to demonstrate good awareness and quick decision making to maintain possession under pressure.
2. When a player in a corner zone receives the ball, the team in possession need to make good supporting angled movements to the left and right to receive the first time pass.
3. Limit the players to 2 touches to speed up play and the decision making.

David Aznar Spanish Football Federation Youth Development Coach

Quick Finishing 4 Goals Possession Game   20 min

Objective
To develop possession play and finishing.

Description
We use the area in between both penalty areas and play a 10v10 game again. There are 2 goalkeepers defending 4 goals in the centre (goals are positioned as shown).

One team must try and score as many goals as possible within a set amount of time (e.g. 2 minutes as shown in diagram) while the other team defends. If the defending team win the ball, they must then try and retain possession for the remainder of the time.

The players are not allowed to enter the centre circle where the goals are (except for the goalkeepers). If the goalkeeper collects (saves) the ball, he must give it to the opposing team.

Coaching Points
1. Players should shoot whenever they have a yard of space.
2. Passes need to be fast and accurate to work positions to shoot.
3. Strategies to find balance between covering goals and winning possession of the ball should be created by the defending team.

David Aznar Spanish Football Federation Youth Development Coach

One-Two Combination Support Play in an 8 v 8 (+2) Possession Game

15 min

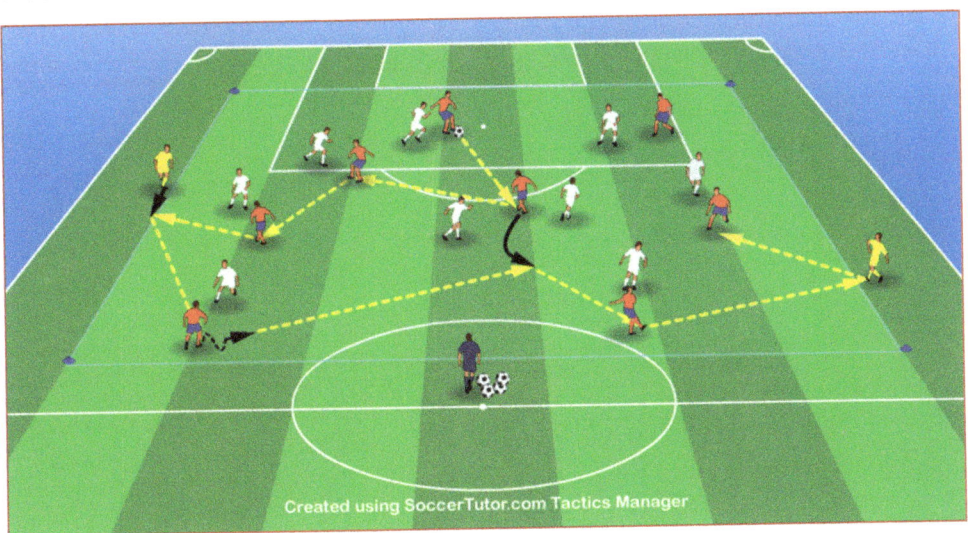

Objective
To develop possession play with a focus on support movements and passing/receiving.

Description
Using half a full sized pitch, we have a zone marked out (as shown).

The players within the zone (9v9) have unlimited touches and the 2 outside neutral players (yellow) are limited to 2 touches. The neutral players play with the team in possession.

To score a point, the team in possession must play a one-two combination with both neutral players without the defending team touching the ball.

Coaching Points
1. The correct angles and distances for support play are required and should be monitored.
2. At least 2 players need to provide an immediate passing option for the neutral player (left and right of him).
3. All players need to keep moving, especially when attempting to receive from a neutral.

David Aznar Spanish Football Federation Youth Development Coach

Possession Play with a 7 v 9 Numerical Disadvantage Transition Game

20 min

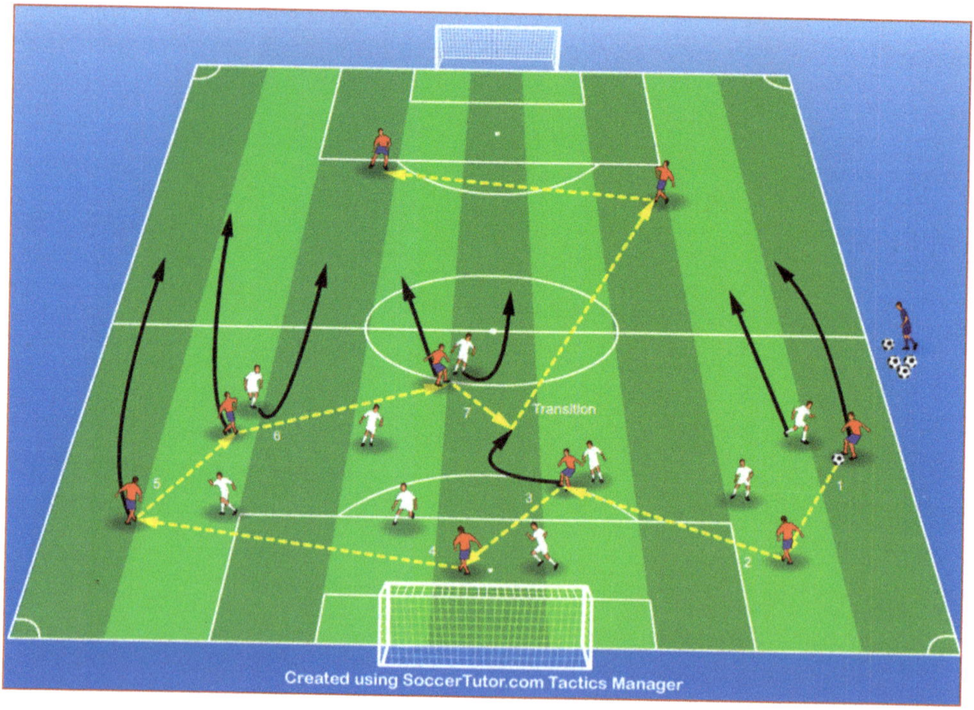

Objective
To develop possession with a numerical advantage and quick reactions in the transition phase.

Description
For this transition game we use a full pitch and have 2 teams of 9 players.

The team in possession (reds) starts with 7 players in one half against 9 opposition players and must complete at least 6 consecutive passes with every player touching the ball before they can pass to their 2 teammates in the other half.

If the ball is intercepted by the whites, 2 white players swap positions with the 2 reds in the other half. The whites then have the same possession aim with a 7v9 disadvantage.

Coaching Points
1. The focus here is on keeping possession under pressure and with a numerical disadvantage, so players need to be constantly moving and must pass the ball at a high tempo.
2. The defending team should use good ball oriented defence to try and win the ball (collective pressing).

David Aznar Spanish Football Federation Youth Development Coach

8 v 8 One-Two Combination Side Zone SSG   *15 min*

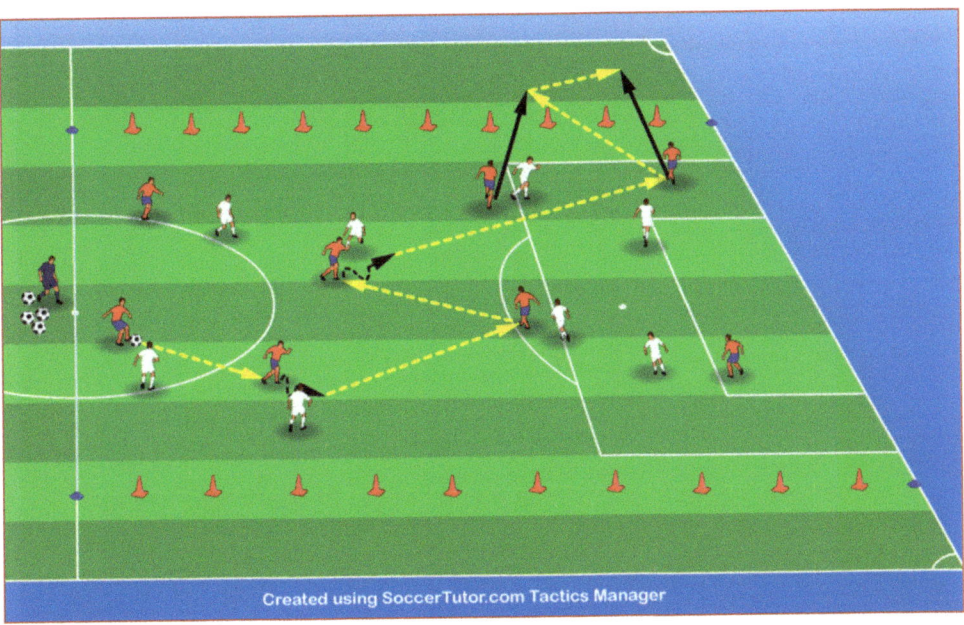

Objective
To develop passing, possession, player movement and good combination play (focus on 1-2).

Description
In an area 60 x 50 yards, we play an 8v8 small sided game with both teams able to attack in both directions.

The aim is for 2 players to play a 1-2 combination through the cones into one of the side zones and gain good control of the ball. The player who receives must then pass back to his teammate within the side zone to score a goal.

Coaching Points
1. The weight and timing of the second pass in the 1-2 combination is key so the second player can run onto the ball and receive.
2. The correct body shape should be monitored (opening up) and receiving/passing with the back foot (foot furthest away from the ball).
3. The practice should be executed with 1 touch whenever possible.

David Aznar Spanish Football Federation Youth Development Coach

3 Team Support Play Possession Game

20 min

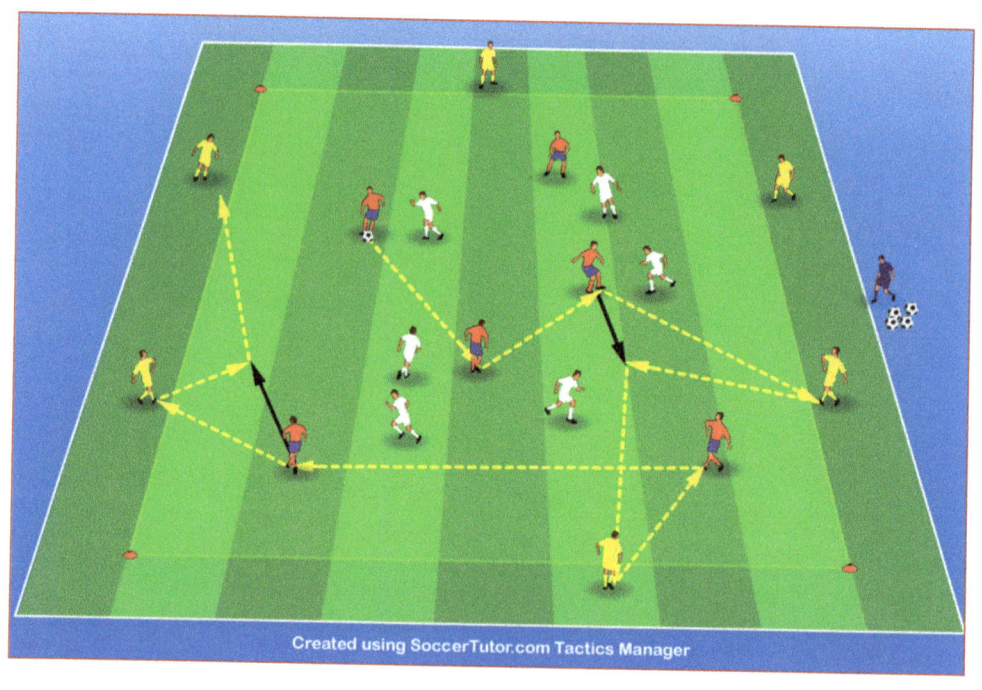

Objective
To develop possession play with a numerical advantage, focusing on support play.

Description
In an area 60 x 45 yards, we have 3 teams of 6 players. There are 2 teams inside and 1 team outside to provide support (players are in positions shown). The outside team play with the team in possession.

To score a point/goal, the team in possession must play a 1-2 combination with 2 support players consecutively on opposite sides of the area. This must be without the ball being intercepted by the opposing team.

Every so often, change the roles by moving a different team outside to provide the support.

Coaching Points
1. The correct body shape should be monitored (opening up) and receiving/passing with the back foot (foot furthest away from the ball).
2. Players should vary their passes - passes to feet and passes into space.
3. Collective pressing (with good defensive shape) is key to trying to win the ball from the opposition.

Quick One-Two End to End Possession Game   20 min

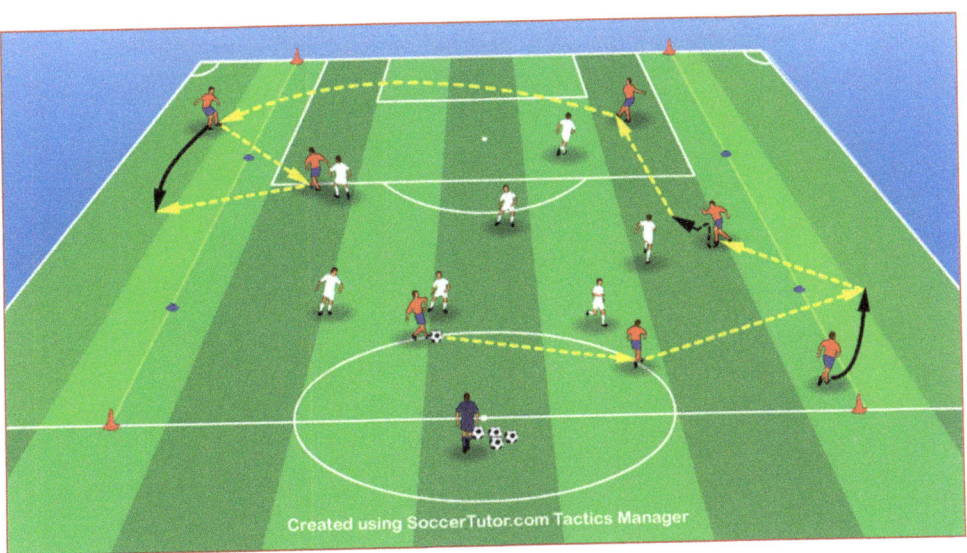

Objective
To develop possession play with a focus on 1-2 combinations and player movement.

Description
We use half a pitch and mark out 3 zones as shown in the diagram. This creates 2 end zones in the areas near the sidelines. 2 teams (7v7) play with unlimited touches in the central zone.

To score a point, the team in possession must pass the ball into an end zone for a player who moves in there. A 1-2 combination must be played and the team retain possession. The team then repeat the action towards the opposite end zone.

The defending team can enter the penalty area to defend, but if they win the ball they must clear it from the zone with just 1 touch.

Coaching Points
1. You can make this practice position specific with the teams in a 4-2-1 or 2-4-1 formation with the full backs or wingers being the ones to move into the side zones.
2. This exercise makes the players move quickly to support their teammates in wide positions as they must play a 1-2 combination.

David Aznar Spanish Football Federation Youth Development Coach

Passing through the Lines with Support Play in a 3 Team End to End Possession Game

15 min

Objective
To develop passing though the lines (defence or midfield) and maintaining possession with support play.

Description
Using half a full sized pitch, we have 3 teams of 7 players in 3 different zones (as shown). The teams on the outside try to pass the ball between each other without the team in the middle intercepting it.

The teams on the outside can have 1 support player in the central zone, but the same player is not allowed to be there all of the time, so must interchange with other players on their team.

The roles of each team can be changed at any time or when the team in the centre win the ball.

Coaching Points
1. The correct angles and distances for the support player should be monitored.
2. The team in the middle need to coordinate and create the correct shapes to be able to block possible passing options/lanes.

David Aznar Spanish Football Federation Youth Development Coach

4 Zone Dynamic Possession, Transition Play and Pressing Game

15 min

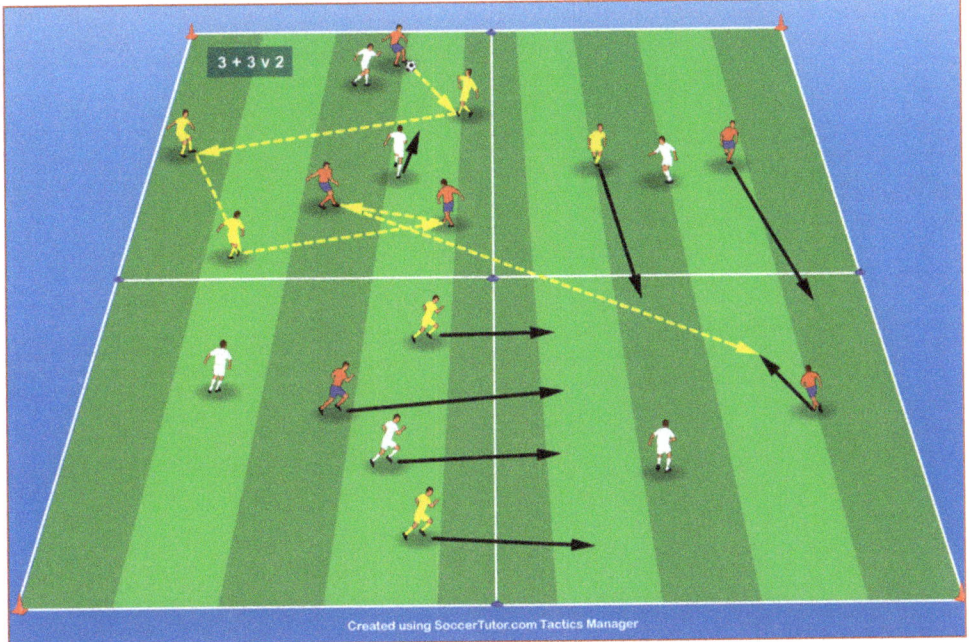

Objective
To develop passing, possession, player movement, pressing and transition play.

Description
In an area 40 x 40 yards, we divide the pitch into 4 equal zones. We play with 3 teams of 6 players. The game starts in one zone with 2 teams in possession of the ball in a 3+3 v 2 situation. In the diagram, the 2 white players try to win the ball from the other 6 players.

The other players are all moving freely across the other 3 zones. As soon as 5 consecutive passes are completed in 1 zone, the ball is passed to a teammate in another zone. Immediately, the other players move into this zone to create another 3+3 v 2 situation.

If the whites win the ball, they continue in possession and the team that lost the ball becomes the defending team. The objectives remain the same.

Coaching Point
The focus here is on the player's quick reactions to the varying game situations.

8 v 8 Support Play Possession Game

15 min

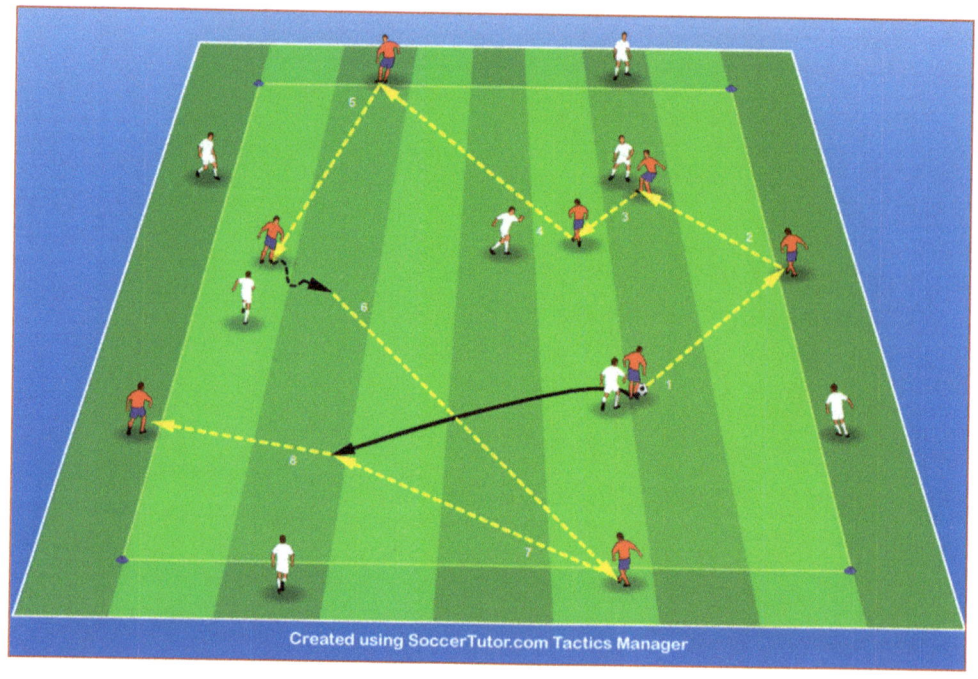

Objective
To develop possession play with a focus on support movements and passing/receiving.

Description
In a 25 yard square, we have 2 teams of 8 players.

Within the zone, we have a 4v4 situation. Both teams have an additional 4 players with 1 player on each side of the square who provide support.

For the team in possession to score a point, the ball must be played to each of the support players without the opposing team intercepting. If the defending team win the ball, they continue with the same aim.

Coaching Points
1. The correct angles and distances for the support player should be monitored.
2. The correct body shape should be monitored (opening up) and receiving/passing with the back foot (foot furthest away from the ball).

Practices to Improve Finishing

David Aznar Spanish Football Federation Youth Development Coach

4 v 4 Create Space and Finishing Small Sided Game 20 min

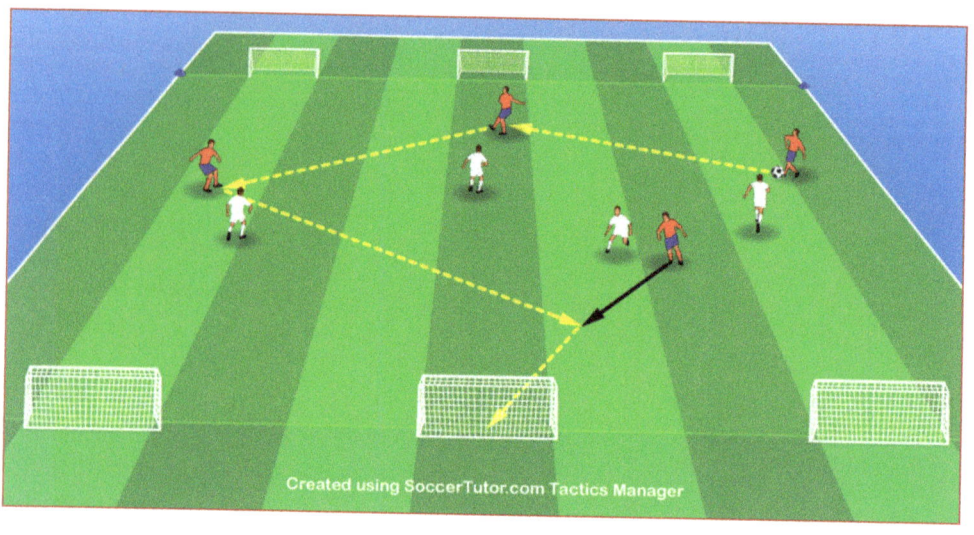

Objective
To develop vision and awareness to create space and finishing.

Description
In an area 50 x 60 yards, we play a 4v4 game between 2 teams that attack and defend 3 goals.

The focus of this game is on the good use of space (making sure to use the full width and length of the area) so the players are able to create opportunities to shoot and score.

Variations
1. Limit the touches each player can take.
2. Introduce neutral players.

Coaching Points
1. Players need to be constantly moving and should avoid crowding around the ball at all costs.
2. Players should check away from their marker before moving to receive in space.
3. Focus on the accuracy of the finishing (not the power) as there are no goalkeepers.

David Aznar Spanish Football Federation Youth Development Coach

Quick Counter Attack with Wide Support Play in a 4 Goals Small Sided Game

25 min

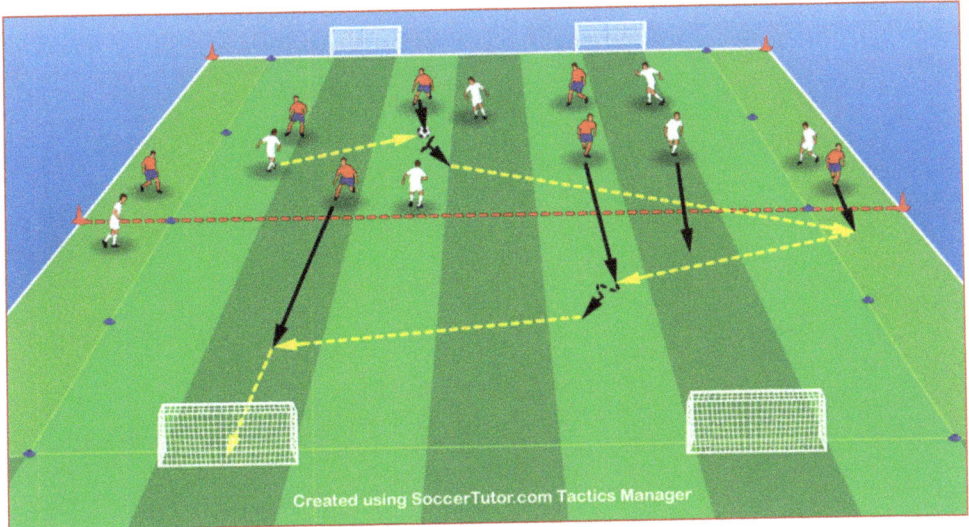

Objective
To develop possession and finishing with wide support play.

Description
In an area 50 x 60 yards, 2 teams (5v5) attack and defend 2 goals. There are 2 additional players for each team situated in 4 side zones as shown (5 x 30 yards each).

One team starts in possession and attack 2 goals (with the use of their wide players).

If the defending team wins the ball, they should play a pass out wide to one of their teammates in the side zone and mount a quick counter attack. An example of a quick counter attack is shown in the diagram.

Coaching Points
1. There should be a rapid transition from attack to defence.
2. Make sure the player that intercepts the ball does not hang onto it, but releases the ball quickly.
3. Players should should try to finish the attack as quickly as possible (shoot quickly).

David Aznar Spanish Football Federation Youth Development Coach

Accurate Through Ball and Finishing in a 4 v 3 Attack **30 min**

Objective
To develop passing in the final third, support play and finishing.

Description
Using half a full sized pitch, we place 4 small cone gates (5-8 yards apart) across the pitch as shown. 4 players attack (2 wide) and 3 defend (+ goalkeeper).

The attackers must pass the ball through 1 of the gates in order to then be able to attack the main goal. The defenders try to stop the attacking team from scoring, first by defending the cone gates and then by defending the main goal with the goalkeeper. There is no offside rule.

Variations
1. Limit the amount of touches until they pass through a cone gate.
2. If the defenders win the ball they attack (with aim to dribble past the halfway line).

Coaching Points
1. This should be run at a fast pace with changes of direction and many 2 on 1 situations.
2. Make sure the wide players do not play too far from the goal.

David Aznar Spanish Football Federation Youth Development Coach

Continuous Crossing and Finishing Practice   25 min

Objective
We work on a specific pattern, incorporating the use of wide areas to practice crossing and finishing.

Description
In half a full sized pitch, we have 8 players participating in this practice. We have 4 players starting in the middle (B, C, D & E). The other 4 players (white) are positioned on the end lines and 1 of these players starts with the ball (becomes player A).

Player A passes to player B out wide who passes to C in the middle. Player C plays the ball out wide for B to run onto and cross into the area. After playing the ball, player C sprints into the box to receive the cross, as do D & E. After each phase, rotate the players.

Start the practice immediately from another corner with a different white player A. Start without defenders and then progress by introducing them (as shown in the diagram).

Variations
1. Introduce different combinations and technical actions.
2. Limit the amount of touches the players have and make it a competition (2 teams).

Coaching Points
1. Focus on making sure the drill is dynamic and flows well at a good tempo.
2. Make sure players are constantly moving and avoid being static waiting for the cross.

David Aznar Spanish Football Federation Youth Development Coach

Passing in Behind and Finishing in a 4 v 3 Attack   20 min

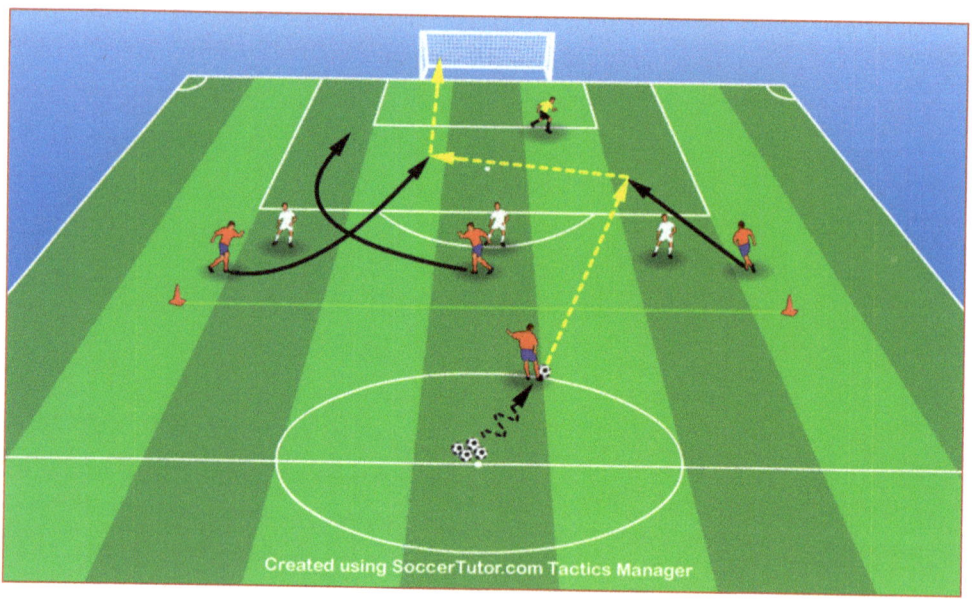

Objective
To improve the quality of forward runs, the ability to escape a marker and passing in behind.

Description
In this practice, 3 attackers (+1 neutral) play against 3 defenders. We place 2 cones to create a line across the pitch 5 yards longer than the width of the penalty area.

The neutral player must stay behind the line and starts with the ball. The aim is to pass the ball in behind the defenders. The 3 attackers aim to run in behind the defenders and score in the goal.

The offside rule is applied throughout. Change the player roles often.

Variation
Make it a competition with 2 teams of 3.

Coaching Points
1. Focus on man to man marking for the 3 defenders of the 3 attackers.
2. Players should avoid being static at any time during this practice.
3. Runs need to be well timed for the pass as the offside rule is applied throughout.

David Aznar Spanish Football Federation Youth Development Coach

Creating Space, Quick Combination Play and Finishing in a 6 v 6 Small Sided Game

25 min

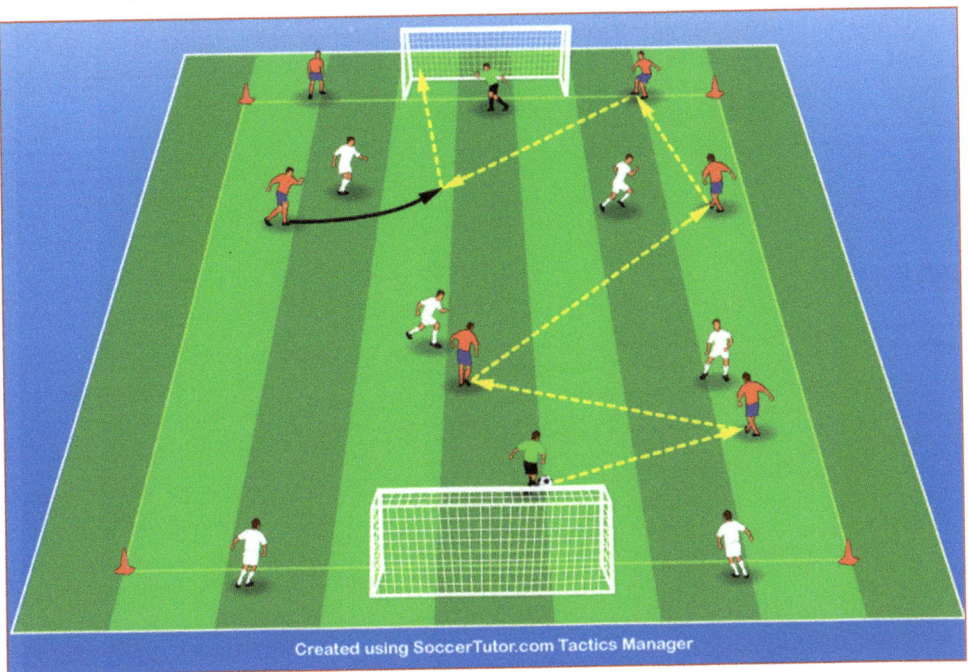

Objective
We work on short combination passing movements followed by a quick finish in a small sided game with support players.

Description
In an area 30 x 35 yards, we have 2 teams of 6 players (+2 goalkeepers). Inside the area, we have a 4v4 situation (players are in a rhombus formation) and each team has 2 support players on the touchline either side of the goal they are attacking.

The objective is to perform short combination passing movements followed by a quick finish.

The players must use man to man marking. We practice losing a marker and outpacing the opponent. The outside players are limited to 1 touch.

Variation
Limit the amount of touches the inside players can take.

David Aznar Spanish Football Federation Youth Development Coach

Escaping a Marker in a 3 Zone Finishing Practice   20 min

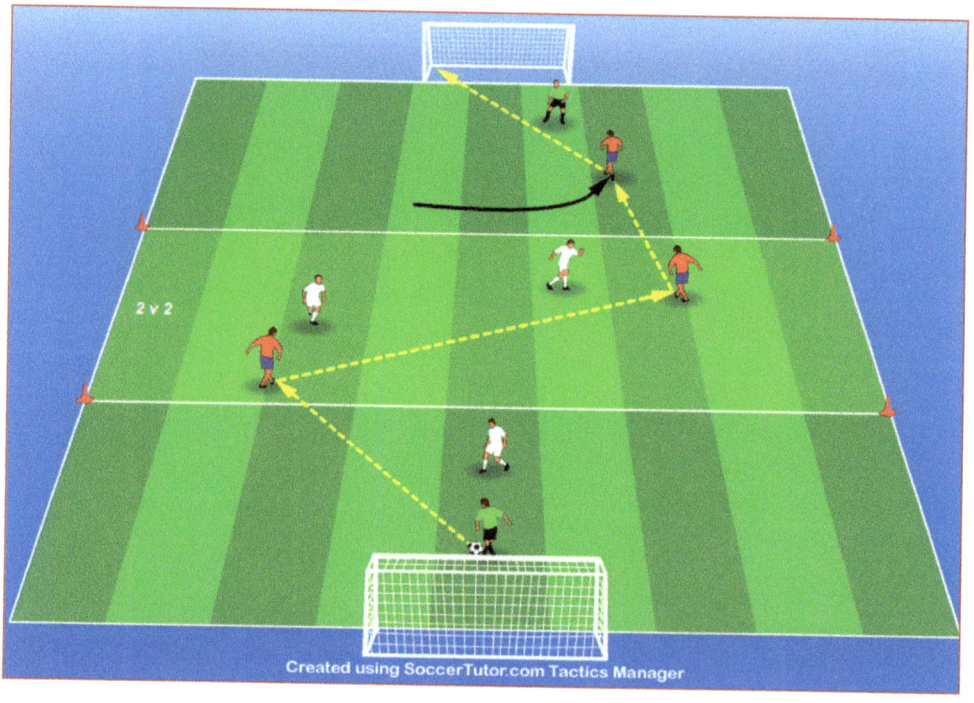

Objective
We work with attackers on escaping their marker and finishing.

Description
In an area double the size of the penalty box, we have a 3v3 situation (+ goalkeepers) with 3 equal zones. It is 2v2 in the central zone with 1 extra player for each team in the outer zones.

A goalkeeper starts the practice and passes the ball into the central zone. From there, the player who receives must look for the movement of his teammates, make a decision who to play the ball to and the team try to score in the opposition's goal.

Keep changing the player roles so all of the players practice their finishing.

Variation
Make it a competition with 2 teams e.g. the first team to score 5 goals win.

Coaching Points
1. Players need to check away from their marker before moving into space to receive.
2. Players should finish with a maximum of 2 touches; 1 to control the ball, another to shoot.
3. Monitor the correct technique for shooting; head over ball, foot through middle of ball.

David Aznar Spanish Football Federation Youth Development Coach

Escaping a Marker and Finishing in a 4 v 4 (+2) Small Sided Game

20 min

Objective
We work with attackers on escaping their marker and finishing in a small sided game.

Description
In an area double the size of the penalty box, we play 3v3 (+ 2 neutral players & 2 goalkeepers). The neutral players play with the team in possession.

In this small area, the players should look to shoot before the 4th pass. They have 2 neutral players to help them create space more easily and they should take the shot as quickly as possible.

Coaching Points
1. The team in possession needs to exploit the numerical advantage to create space to shoot.
2. Running into space is the key here, losing your marker to receive the pass.
3. Speed up play - reduce the time between the first touch and the pass or shot.

CHAPTER 2

RAFA JUANES

Villarreal CF Technical Academy Coordinator and former Atlético Madrid Coach

VILLARREAL CF TECHNICAL ACADEMY COORDINATOR PROFILE

Rafa Juanes
Villarreal CF Head Technical Academy Coordinator

Previous Coaching positions:
- Atlético Madrid Academy Coach

Credentials:
- UEFA A Licence
- National team trainer (technical coach)

RAFA JUANES Villarreal CF Technical Academy Coordinator

SPECIAL PROGRAM DESIGNED FOR TECHNICAL IMPROVEMENT IN TACTICAL POSITIONING

Introduction

When looking at the current demands of the sport and the high level of competition required, we see the underlying need for the specific educational development of young football players to improve their performance and athletic ability through practice.

Following on from this idea, there is a need for a special work program that serves to solve the technical problems that routinely occur in every game and are conditioned by the player's different positions.

The program that we propose is based on our experience in developing players between the ages of 10 and 20 years old over 3 seasons at an elite Spanish football club.

Prior Conditions

The program that we suggest is structured around the following tactical positioning outline:

- Central defenders
- Wide players
- Central midfielders
- Forwards

For each of the positions we create both attacking and defensive situations aimed at the implementation and development of specific techniques.

The situations on which we will work, which must be different so as to be defined as "special", arise from situations that a player is faced with during a game. These include conditions of space, time, positioning and the opposition, who are faced with similar situations of their own and therefore must also be studied.

It is important to state that the program which we will present should in no way replace the usual training, but should be used to complement it.

RAFA JUANES Villareal CF Technical Academy Coordinator

CHARACTERISTICS OF THE WORK

SPATIAL ORIENTATION	Show the player their positioning in relation to the ball, the opposition and their teammates.
TEMPORAL ORIENTATION	Show the player the time he has to execute an action successfully, always referring to the opposition positioning.
PHYSICAL OPPOSITION	Taking the previous characteristics into account, explain how the player's body should be positioned in order to gain an advantage.
TECHNICAL MOVEMENT	An important aspect of the program is the repetition of the technical movement in order to mechanise the players to perform the same responses to a problem and in the same order.
TACTICAL ANSWERS	Take into account that all of the actions include a tactical element that must be interlinked.

RAFA JUANES Villareal CF Technical Academy Coordinator

ACTIONS ON WHICH TO WORK

The development of each of the techniques that can be improved has been included according to specific tactical positioning.

Depending on the relevance and specific application within the whole team and the individual progression of each footballer, we propose that the work is developed based on the following principles:

1. PASSES

- Long
- Effective

2. CONTROL

- Cushioning
- Directional control (including controlling the ball after a feint)

3. INDIVIDUAL ACTIONS

- Dribbling and passing
- Dribbling and dummying
- Dummies

4. HEADING GAMES

- Defensive actions
- Team actions
- Heading on goal

5. TECHNICAL DEFENSIVE ACTIONS

- Anticipation and interception
- Clearing (including directed clearances)
- Tackling

6. SHOOTING

These principles are all generic. The focus of each of the actions should be drawn from specific game situations and transferred onto the training ground.

RAFA JUANES Villareal CF Technical Academy Coordinator

DEVELOPMENT OF THE PROGRAM: CENTRE BACKS

In this section we look at the development of technical training specific to **centre backs**.

The program we suggest was intended for central backs and a back 4 that plays with zonal marking. However, the proposed actions are not exclusive, but are those that we believe are indispensable to the development of a footballer and are based on the style of play implemented at the certain football club from which we have created this program.

We are sure that this program can be adapted to suit the different styles of different teams.

When looking at and evaluating the different practices we have to take into account the skills outlined in the following diagram.

Depending on the generic method already used, the actions that we must develop and improve are as follows:

PASSES	Forward passes and short diagonal passes (Both with and without opposition).
CONTROL	Close control and directional control. Controlled interceptions and cushioning the ball.
INDIVIDUAL ACTIONS	Short runs with temporal and spatial orientation.
DEFENSIVE HEADING	Jumping forward heading from a standing position, jumping forward heading on the run, heading forwards to support player, sideways lateral headers to a teammate whilst on the run and static lateral headers with opposition.
ATTACKING HEADING	Passes, throw-ins, lateral headers (both static and moving) and flick-ons.
TECHNICAL DEFENSIVE ACTIONS	Frontal tackles (technique and timing), sliding tackles, reflexive anticipation, anticipations, clearing and directive clearances.

PRACTICAL APPLICATION

When developing and evaluating the execution of the different exercises, we have to take the following into account:

SPECIFIC ELEMENTS	CONDITIONS
Spatial orientation	As similar as possible to reality
Physical imbalances	Situational analysis (from part to the whole)
Protection and physical opposition	Use real actions
Dominant leg	Strong and real opposition
Reading of tactical references	Evaluate temporal and spatial orientation
Decision making	Precise application to the game, not just learning through drills
Mechanisation of technical movements	

RAFA JUANES Villareal CF Technical Academy Coordinator

Tracking Back, Intercepting and Building up Play with a Long Diagonal Ball

20 min

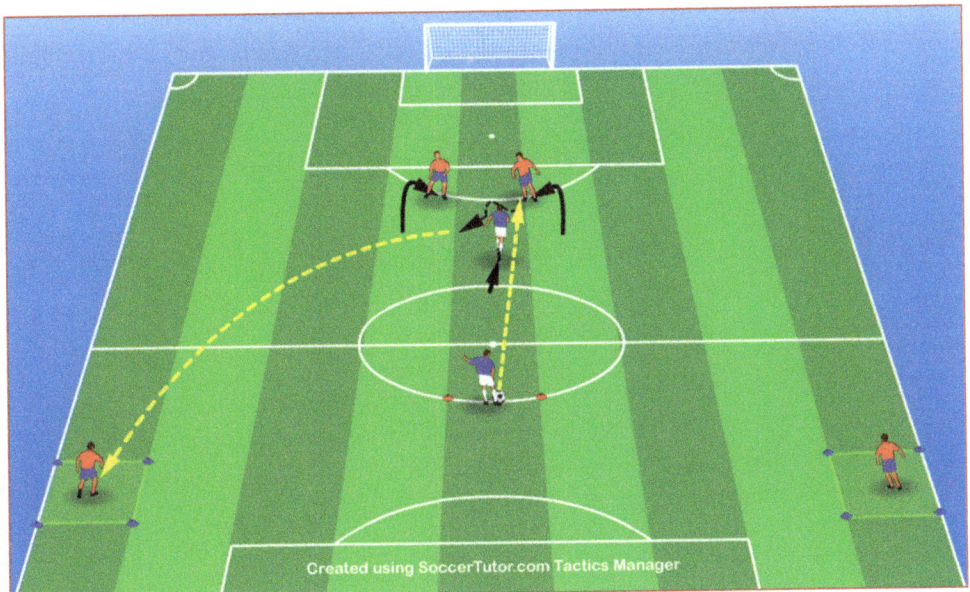

Objective
We work with the defenders on tracking back, intercepting and playing out from the back.

Description
In this exercise, we work with 6 players. The practice starts with a deep forward pass from an opponent (blue), either in the air or along the ground.

The red defenders move back together, one of them intercepts and controls the ball (under pressure from the opponent), makes a short run forward and plays a diagonal pass to a teammate on the flank on the opposite side.

Coaching Points

1. Emphasise the correct positioning within the defensive line, depending on the position of the ball and teammates.
2. Be aware of the player's positioning and movement when tracking back.
3. Propose which direction to play the ball after the interception, depending on the position of the closest opponent.
4. Dribble and pass the ball using the opposite foot to the side that is put under pressure.

RAFA JUANES Villareal CF Technical Academy Coordinator

Directing Headed Clearances from a Long Ball   20 min

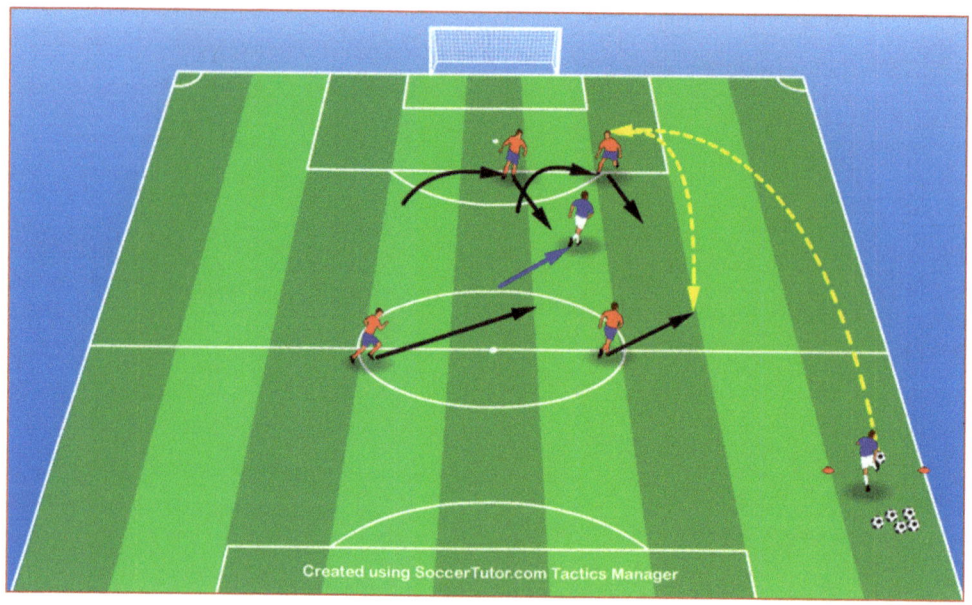

Objective
We work with the centre backs on directed clearances from a long ball.

Description
We work with 6 players again. The practice starts with a long ball from an opponent (blue), the red defenders move back together and the other blue opponent applies pressure.

The aim for the defender is to head the ball away, directing it to one of their teammates (midfielders). This is a coordinated clearance which allows the team to then move forward.

Coaching Points
1. Emphasise the correct positioning within the defensive line, depending on the position of the ball and teammates.
2. Players need to be aware of their positioning and movement when tracking back.
3. Make the players aware of the type of defensive header necessary; heading the bottom of the ball to get height in the clearance or leaving the ball in the air for longer, giving a teammate more time to collect the ball.
4. Make sure the defenders are facing forwards at all times.

RAFA JUANES Villareal CF Technical Academy Coordinator

Defensive Covering on the Flank and Challenging for the Ball

20 min

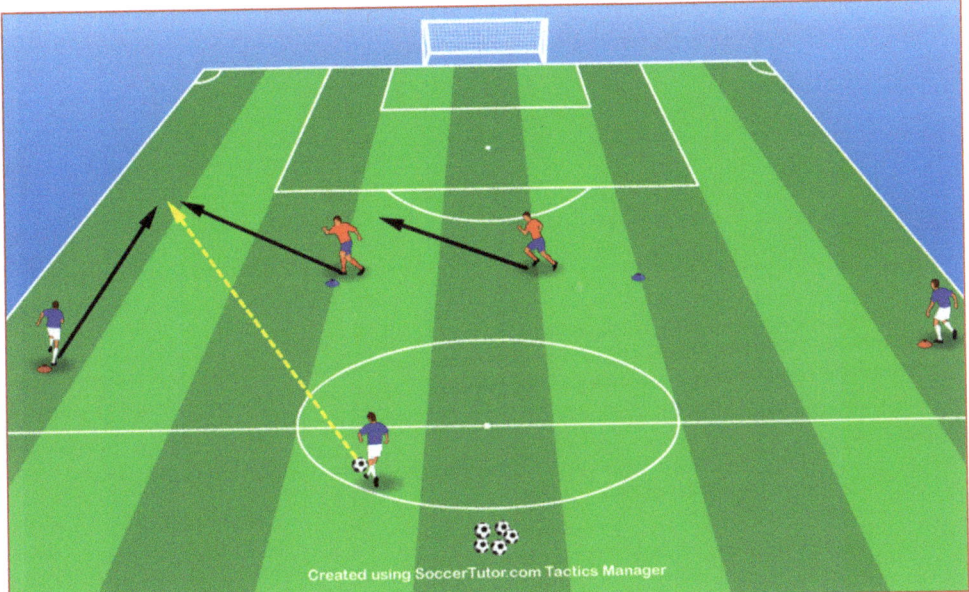

Objective
We work on defensive covering (centre backs) for an attack on the flank.

Description
We work with 4 players. The practice starts with a pass down the line from one blue player to the other as shown. The red defenders move across to apply pressure on the ball.

The defender should use their shoulder to pressure the attacker and try to make contact with the ball after a legal challenge. As soon as the defender wins the ball, repeat the practice.

Coaching Points
1. Emphasise the correct positioning within the defensive line, depending on the position of the ball and teammates.
2. The defenders should use their body to try and nudge the player off the ball if they are unable to make contact with it.
3. Look for the run rather than at the ball. Also, look for the trajectory of the opponent's run in order to intercept the ball or put the opponent under pressure when receiving.

RAFA JUANES Villareal CF Technical Academy Coordinator

Defending Set Pieces with Opposed Man to Man Marking

20 min

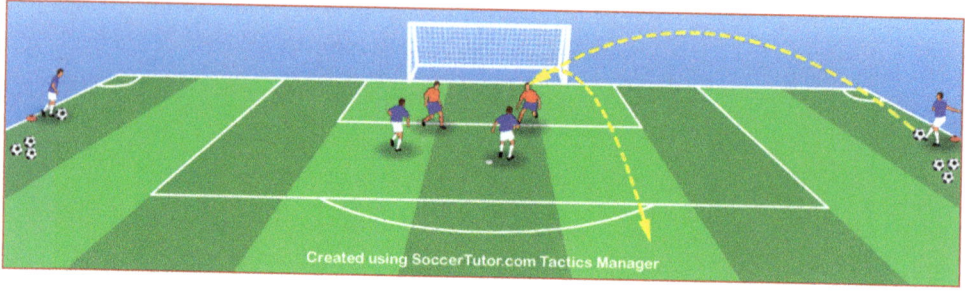

Objective
We work with the centre backs on defending set pieces.

Description
In this exercise, we work with 5 players. 1 player crosses a high, hanging ball from the sideline.

The 2 defenders (red) aim to head the ball clear, while the attackers try to score in the goal.

Start with static defensive headers and progress to the attackers moving more, making the defenders head the ball clear on the move.

Coaching Points
1. Emphasise the need for the correct positioning and body shape of the defenders.
2. We want strong defensive headers in this exercise.
3. Evaluate the header, making sure contact was made with the correct part of the head and ball.
4. Make sure there is some physical contact with the opponent.

RAFA JUANES Villareal CF Technical Academy Coordinator

Defending a High Long Ball with Headed Clearances

20 min

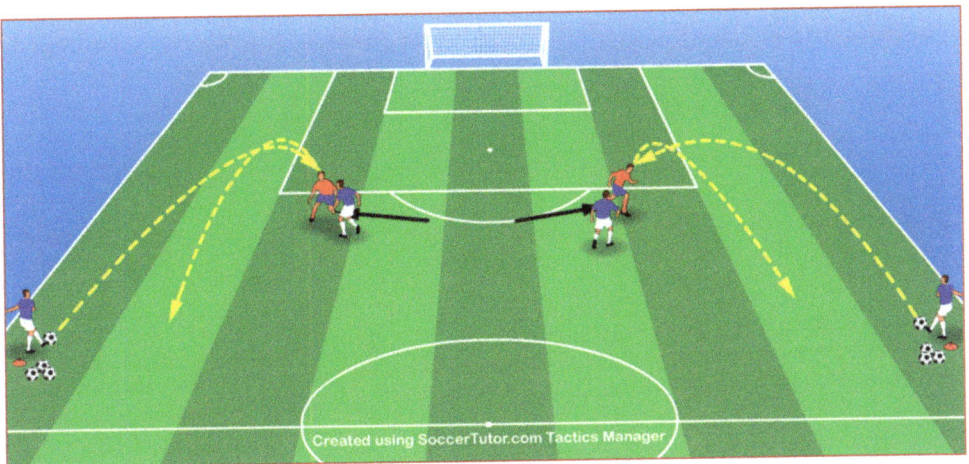

Objective
We work with the centre backs on defensive headers from a high ball.

Description
In this exercise, we work with 6 players. 2 players cross a high, hanging ball from the sideline towards the edge of the penalty area simultaneously.

Both defenders (red) are put under pressure by one of the blue attackers and have to head them ball clear.

Coaching Points
1. We want strong defensive headers in this exercise with good height for the clearance.
2. Emphasise the need for the correct positioning and body shape of the defenders.
3. Evaluate the header, making sure contact was made with the correct part of the head and ball.
4. Make sure there is some physical contact with the opponent.

RAFA JUANES Villareal CF Technical Academy Coordinator

SPECIAL PROGRAM TO DEVELOP TECHNICAL PERFECTION THROUGH TACTICAL POSITIONING: WIDE PLAYERS

Program Development

In this second section, we look at the development of technical training specifically for wide players (full backs and wingers/wide midfielders).

As stated before, although this is based on the style of play implemented at the certain football club from which we have created this program, we are sure that this program can be adapted to suit the different styles of different teams.

When looking at and evaluating the different drills we have to take into account the skills outlined in the following diagram.

Depending on the generic method already used, the actions that we must develop and improve are as follows:

PASSES	CONTROL	INDIVIDUAL ACTIONS	DEFENSIVE HEADING	ATTACKING HEADING	TECHNICAL ACTIONS
Parallel passes down the line. Practice with passive opposition.	Controlling the ball and directional control.	Short run and pass.	Jumping forwards header.	Passes	Anticipation
Long diagonal passes.	Controlled interceptions.	Dummying, dribbling and passing on the run with aggressive opposition.	Lateral headers in the opposite direction from the run.	Shots, lateral headers (both static and moving), with and without opposition.	Side on running tackles wide players only, not tackling from behind as there will be players covering).
Passing on the run, with aggressive opposition.	Cushioned control.	Dribbling and dummying while running at speed.	Static lateral headers with opposition.		Frontal tackles (body position/shape and timing).
Diagonal passes after dribbling, usually with the opposite foot.	Cushioning the ball on the run.	Complex dummies, look for diversity in a limited space and execution with both feet.	Heading to a support player.		Clearing the ball away with distance and directed clearances.
Passing the ball around the opposition and chasing, usually after a dummy.	Cushioning, dribbling and dummying.				

RAFA JUANES Villareal CF Technical Academy Coordinator

PRACTICAL APPLICATION

When developing and evaluating the execution of the different exercises we have to take the following into account:

SPECIFIC ELEMENTS	CONDITIONS
Spatial orientation	As similar as possible to reality
Physical imbalances	Situational analysis (from part to the whole)
Protection and physical opposition	Use real actions
Dominant leg	Strong and real opposition
Reading of tactical references	Evaluate temporal and spatial orientation
Decision making	Precise application to the game, not just learning through drills
Mechanisation of technical movements	

Playing Across the Back and a Full Back's Long Pass for Forward

20 min

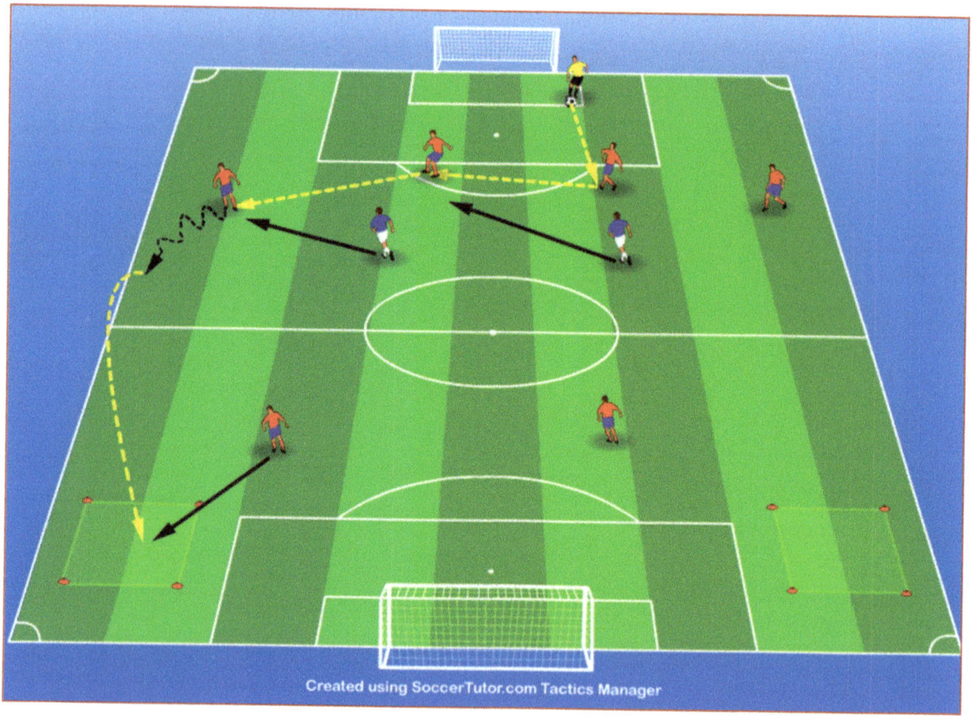

Objective
We work on building up play from the back under pressure from the opposition.

Description
This is a tactical exercise in working the ball up the pitch from the back and into the opposition half under pressure from 2 opposition forwards.

Start the exercise with a short goal kick and use close control, short runs forward from the full backs, followed by a long pass up the line and into the other half (for a forward).

Coaching Points
1. Receive with the inside of the foot that is not under pressure from the opposition.
2. When running with the ball, use an arm to protect yourself from an opponent.
3. Long passes should be with the foot not under pressure from the opposition (instep or laces).
4. The objective of the pass is to achieve the maximum possible distance so the leg should follow through the pass with perfect body balance.

RAFA JUANES Villareal CF Technical Academy Coordinator

Playing Across the Back and a Full Back's Long Diagonal Pass

20 min

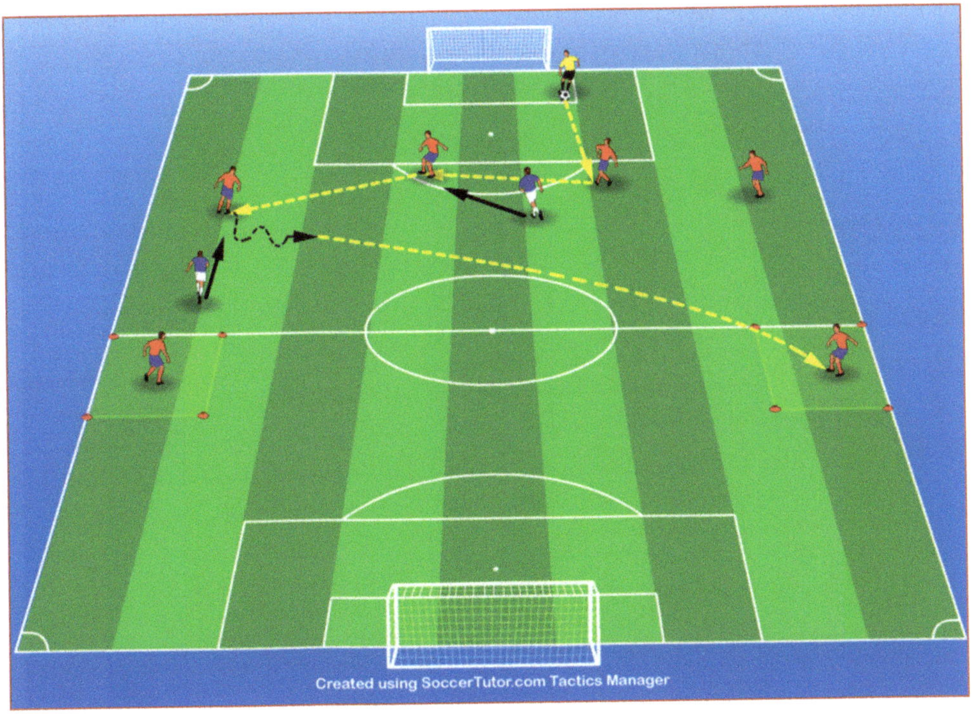

Objective
We work on building up from the back under pressure from the opposition.

Description
This is a tactical exercise to practice working the ball up the pitch from the back and into the opposition half under pressure from 2 opposition forwards.

Start the exercise with a short goal kick and use close control, a short run inside from the full back, followed by a long diagonal pass with the weaker foot to a teammate in the opposition's half.

Coaching Points
1. Receive with the inside of the foot that is not under pressure from the opposition.
2. When running with the ball, use an arm to protect yourself from an opponent.
3. When executing a pass with the weaker foot, you usually see a more mechanical movement with the supporting leg further away than usual from the ball to control the slowing down of the striking leg after making contact with the ball and helping direct it better.

RAFA JUANES Villareal CF Technical Academy Coordinator

Playing the Ball Along the Defensive Line to Switch the Point of Attack

20 min

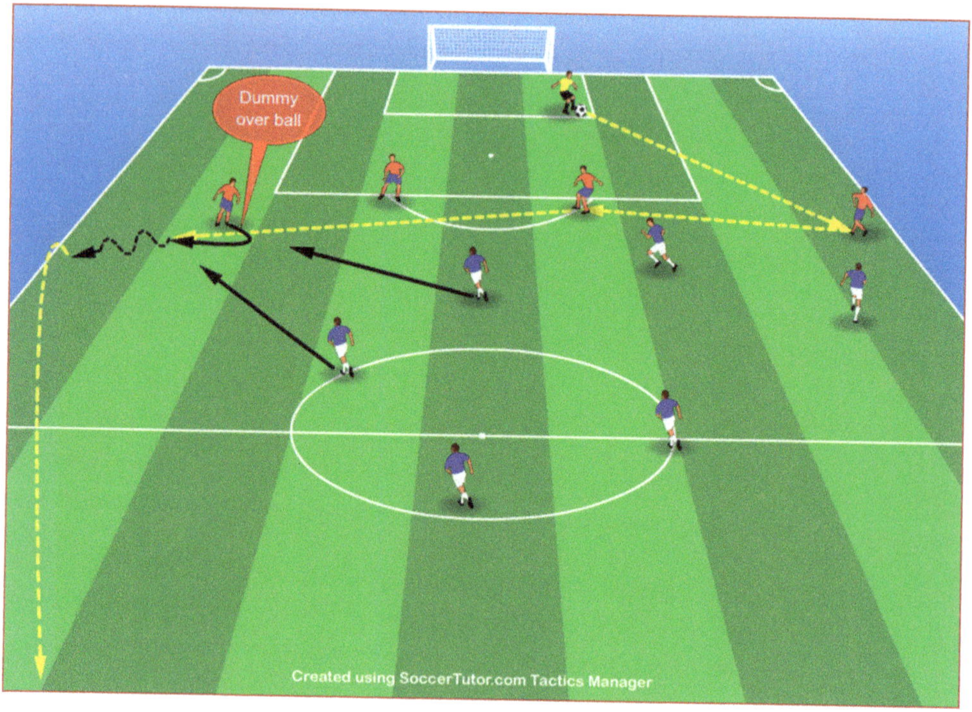

Objective
This is a tactical exercise in playing the ball out of defence under pressure from opponents across the defensive line.

Description
This is a tactical exercise in playing the ball along the back across the pitch to play the ball forward. The back 4 are under pressure from the front 6 of the opposition.

Start the exercise with a short goal kick to one of the full backs. The players work the ball to the other full back (including one dummy as shown) who plays a long ball down the line (while dribbling the ball) for a potential forward.

Coaching Points
1. The support player who runs over the ball (dummy) should direct the opposition away with his body position and protect the ball, making the subsequent technical actions easier.
2. When dribbling towards the touchline, protect the ball by positioning the body in between the ball and the opponent that is applying pressure.
3. The final long pass should be struck with the player's back to the opposition and facing the opposite direction to the direction the pass is played (protecting the ball).

©SoccerTutor.com   *Advanced Spanish Academy Coaching*

RAFA JUANES Villareal CF Technical Academy Coordinator

Full Backs: Receive from the Goalkeeper, Short Dribble and Change of Direction

20 min

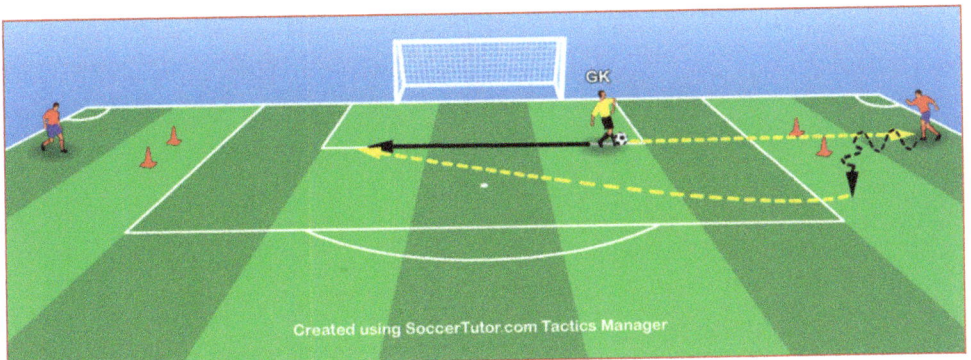

Objective
This is a technical exercise which forms the basis for the correct execution of the practices to follow.

Description
Here we work with 2 defenders (full backs) and a goalkeeper. Start the practice with a short goal kick to one side of the pitch.

The first player to receive sets off with a short run forward, transfers his weight one way and then changes direction past the cones. The player then passes the ball to the goalkeeper who has moved to the corner of the 6 yard box.

The goalkeeper then passes to the other full back and the same sequence is repeated on the other side. The player can make the run inside as well as going outside.

Coaching Point
All contact with the ball should be made with the top of the foot or the instep throughout.

RAFA JUANES Villareal CF Technical Academy Coordinator

Technical Actions for Attacking on the Flank; 1 v 1 Play, Crossing and Finishing

20 min

Objective
We work on the technical action for 1v1 situations on the flank.

Description
One player starts with the ball in the centre and passes to a teammate on the flank who must look at their positioning and find space (check away from their marker) in order to receive the ball in an advantageous area.

The player then has 2 options; dribble to the byline and cross (option A) or dribble inside through the cones and cross (option B) for the 2 forwards in the box.

Progression
Add a defender coming from the side to force the player out wide and stop the cross.

Coaching Points
1. The ball must be crossed by locking the hip and using an internal rotation in the knee.
2. The height and strength of the kick is derived from the speed of movement when the foot makes contact with the ball.
3. The cross must reach the near post at least.

RAFA JUANES Villareal CF Technical Academy Coordinator

Technical Actions for Attacking on the Flank; 1 v 1 Play, Crossing and Finishing (2)

20 min

Objective
We work on the technical action for 1v1 situations on the flank.

Description
One player starts with the ball in the centre and passes to a teammate on the flank who must look at their positioning and find space (check away from their marker) in order to receive the ball in an advantageous area.

This time, the player is faced up with frontal marking by an opponent and must perform a feint or dummy to beat the man.

The player then has the same 2 options again; dribble to the byline and cross (option A) or dribble inside through the cones and cross (option B) for the 2 forwards in the box.

Coaching Point
Once the wide player has gone past the opponent, he should hit a mid range cross while shaping to play a deeper pass (with a long leg extension), allowing the body weight to shift to keep balance.

Attacking on the Flank in 1 v 1 Situations with Switching Play

20 min

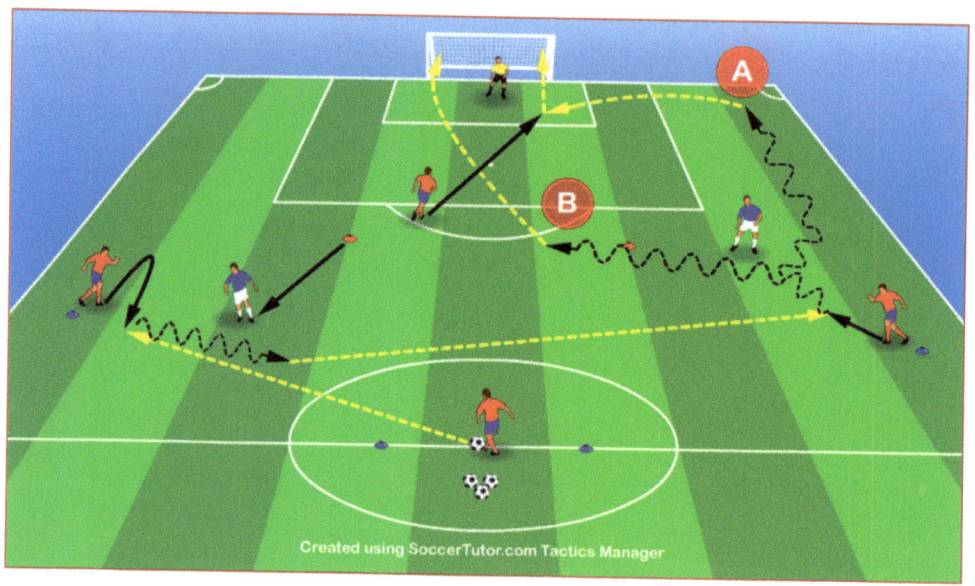

Objective
This practice is used to teach and develop specific movements used by wide players, such as dribbling, dummying and other technical actions.

Description (including Coaching Points)
The ball starts with a red player in the middle. The first tactical action involves the wide player who must lose their marker and move to receive. The player must control and protect the ball.

After controlling the ball, the player must use a feint or dummy from a standing position and use an explosive move inside, before playing a long pass to the other flank.

The second wide player cushions the ball before advancing slowly on the opponent, looking for space and deciding which foot to use to perform a pivot or turn.

The first objective is to make the opponent retreat so that when we change pace and direction, the opponent must also modify their balance and direction which should give us the necessary time and space to gain an advantage.

The practice ends with a cross to the forward or with a shot at goal with the weaker foot.

RAFA JUANES Villareal CF Technical Academy Coordinator

Specific Back 4 Defensive Movements when the Ball is Out Wide

20 min

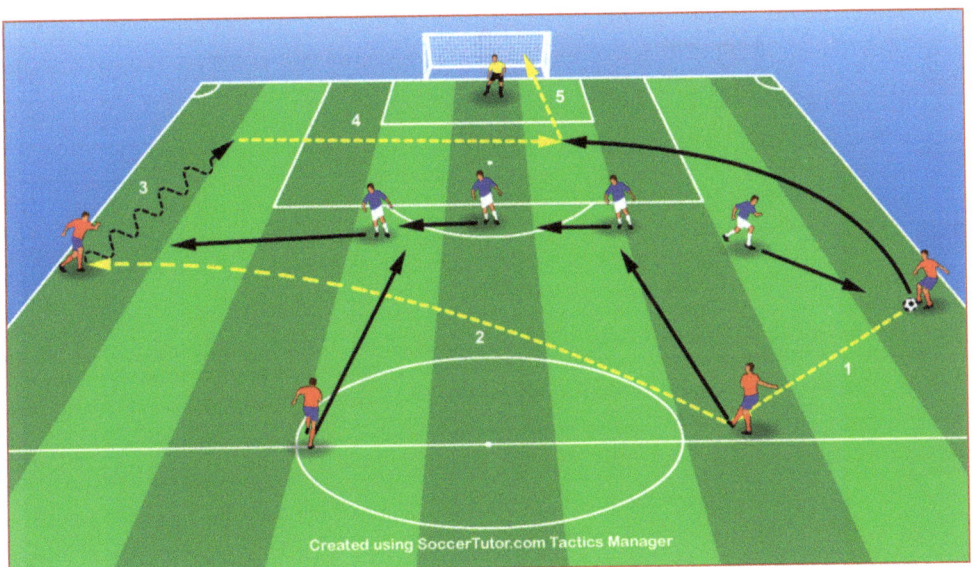

Objective
This practice teaches specific movements used by defenders when the ball is in wide areas.

Description (including Coaching Points)
We play 4v4 and the practice starts with the an attacking wide player (red) as that team work the ball across the pitch. The defensive line moves as one towards the zone where the ball is and must adapt to the change in direction and close in on the opposition.

The initial sideways movement sees the defender pressing to stop the opponent passing. The players need to be able to identify body signals in order to anticipate the opponents movements and when they will strike the ball (cross or shoot).

The defender should aggressively press the opposition to try and retrieve the ball, inviting the player to go wide and not allowing them to come inside to pass to a teammate, making sure the whole defensive line hold their positions.

The practice ends with a cross to the forward or with a shot at goal with the weaker foot.

Variation
Change the defensive players objectives and play more 1v1 and work on the player coming inside where the defensive line should then be able to reduce the opponent's space.

Coaching Points

1. When tracking back, the players should always be facing forwards towards the opposition on the touchline and the head partly turned in the direction of the ball.

2. While pressing the ball carrier, the defender should keep a low centre of gravity so he can stop quickly and anticipate a possible change of direction.

3. When playing in a 1v1 situation, the legs should be slightly bent and kept together and the player should be on his toes so he can quickly shift his body weight, while keeping his torso as straight as possible to facilitate a weight transfer.

RAFA JUANES Villareal CF Technical Academy Coordinator

Tracking Back, Intercepting the Ball and Controlled Defensive Clearances

20 min

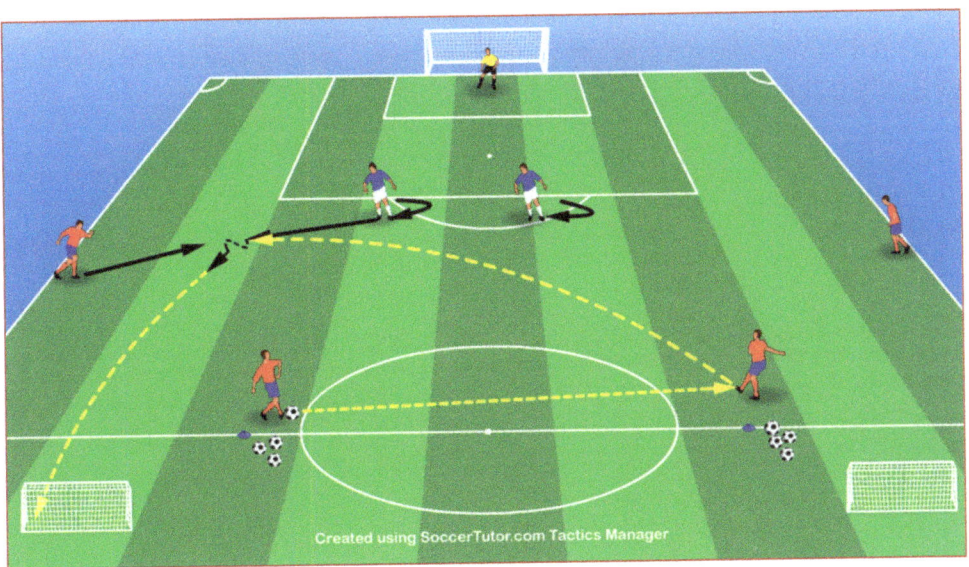

Description
We have a 4v2 situation working with 2 centre backs. The drill starts with the attacking team's centre midfielders and a long diagonal pass to the wide player.

The defenders must be in balanced positions and should respond to the movement and changes in direction of the wide players. The initial sideways movement sees the defender pressing to stop the opponent passing or to intercept the ball (interception shown in diagram).

The players need to be able to identify body signals in order to anticipate the opponent's movements and when they will strike the ball (long pass, cross or shot).

The drill can end with a cross or a shot at goal with the weaker foot. If the ball is played in, the defender should clear the ball with a defensive header in the opposite direction. Alternatively, the defender can intercept the initial pass and aim their clearance into a small goal.

Coaching Point
The clearance technique should be varied depending on the location of the ball when the clearance is made. The clearance can be made with one leg, on the run, or with both legs while either stationary or on the move.

RAFA JUANES Villareal CF Technical Academy Coordinator

SPECIAL PROGRAM TO DEVELOP TECHNICAL PERFECTION THROUGH TACTICAL POSITIONING: CENTRE MIDFIELDERS

Program Development

In the third section we look at the development of technical training specifically for centre **midfielders.**

When looking at and evaluating the different practices we have to take into account the skills outlined in the following diagram.

Depending on the generic method already used, the actions that we must develop and improve are as follows:

PASSES	1. Close control, pass, move forwards, create space to receive. 2. Control after a feint. 3. Control, dummy and pass.
CONTROL	1. Feints and dummies. 2. Feint and movement with temporal and spatial orientation.
INDIVIDUAL ACTIONS	1. Jumping forward header. 2. Directed clearances.
DEFENSIVE HEADING	1. Jumping forward header. 2. Directed clearances.
ATTACKING HEADING	1. Passes. 2. Shots, lateral headers (both static and moving) with and without opposition.
TECHNICAL ACTIONS	1. Profile and timing. 2. Static tackling from behind (anticipation). 3. Lateral tackles. 4. Clearing the ball.

PRACTICAL APPLICATION

When developing and evaluating the execution of the different exercises we have to take the following into account:

SPECIFIC ELEMENTS	CONDITIONS
Spatial orientation	As similar as possible to reality
Physical imbalances	Situational analysis (from part to the whole)
Protection and physical opposition	Use real actions
Dominant leg	Strong and real opposition
Reading of tactical references	Evaluate temporal and spatial orientation
Decision making	Precise application to the game, not just learning through drills
Mechanisation of technical movements	

Coordinated Movements of the Centre Midfielders when Building up Play from the Back

20 min

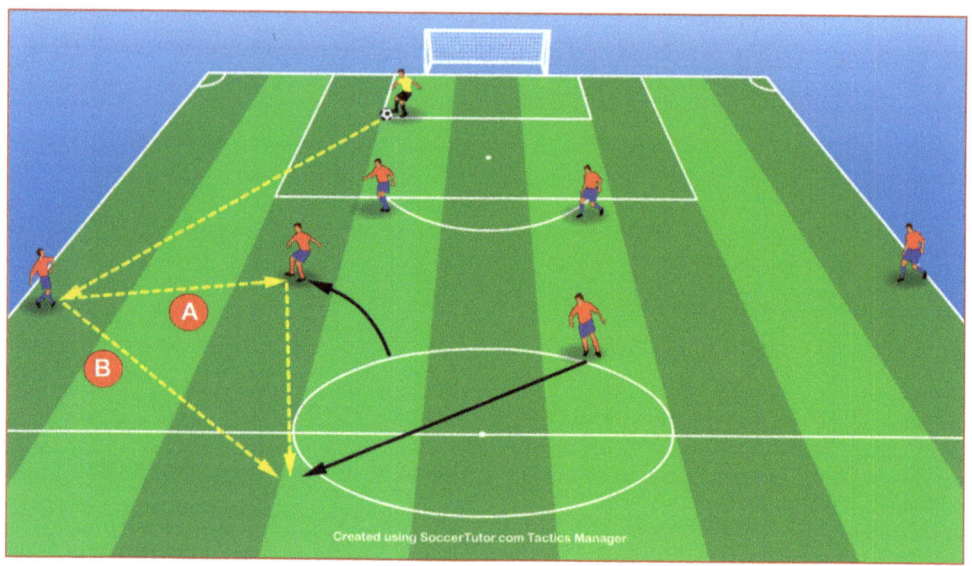

Objective
We work on a tactical situation, coordinating the movement of the 2 centre midfielders when building up from the back.

Description (including Coaching Points)
We work with 2 centre midfielders, the back 4 and a goalkeeper using half a full sized pitch.

Start the practice with a short goal kick. The midfielder nearest the ball should position himself behind the new ball carrier, so he can then see as much of the pitch as possible and be able to make sure that his first touch of the ball can be followed by a positive action.

The centre midfielder should receive the ball with the inside of the foot furthest from the potential opponent. If he has the correct body shape, his first touch can be a pass.

The centre midfielder that is furthest from the ball should make a diagonal movement so the player in possession can play the ball forward and this helps to provide different options. He may also receive directly from the full back (in diagram - option B).

At least 2 passing options must be available to the midfielder for the practice to be considered a success and when the midfielder receives the ball, he should be facing the opposition's half so he has a full field of vision.

Coordinated Movements of the Centre Midfielders when Building up Play from the Back (2)

20 min

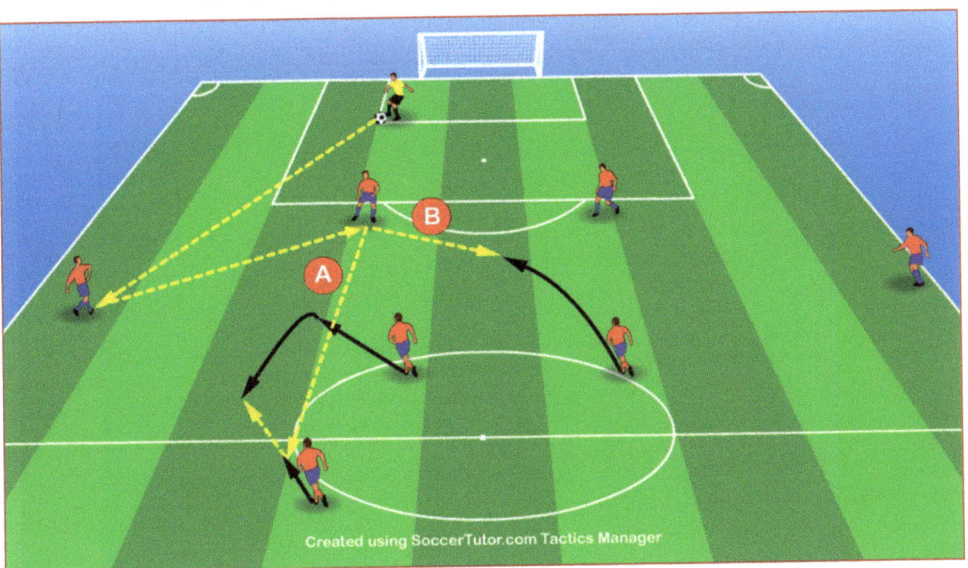

Description (including Coaching Points)

We now add a forward for this pattern of play and again start with a short goal kick. The objective is to receive the ball with an open body to shape to face the opposition's half.

The closest centre midfielder performs the same movement as in the last exercise, but after the pass back to the centre back from the player in possession, he modifies his movement slightly to be in line with the most advanced player in his team. Option A is now a pass to the forward, who can then play the ball back.

The centre midfielder furthest from the ball, upon seeing the decision made by the player in possession (to play the ball backwards to the centre back), moves diagonally inside to offer his teammate an option and receive the ball (option B).

At least 2 passing options must be available to whichever centre midfielder receives the ball for the practice to be considered a success and when the midfielder receives the ball, he should be facing the opposition's half thus having a better field of vision.

RAFA JUANES Villareal CF Technical Academy Coordinator

Coordinated Movements of the Centre Midfielders when Building up Play from the Back (3)

20 min

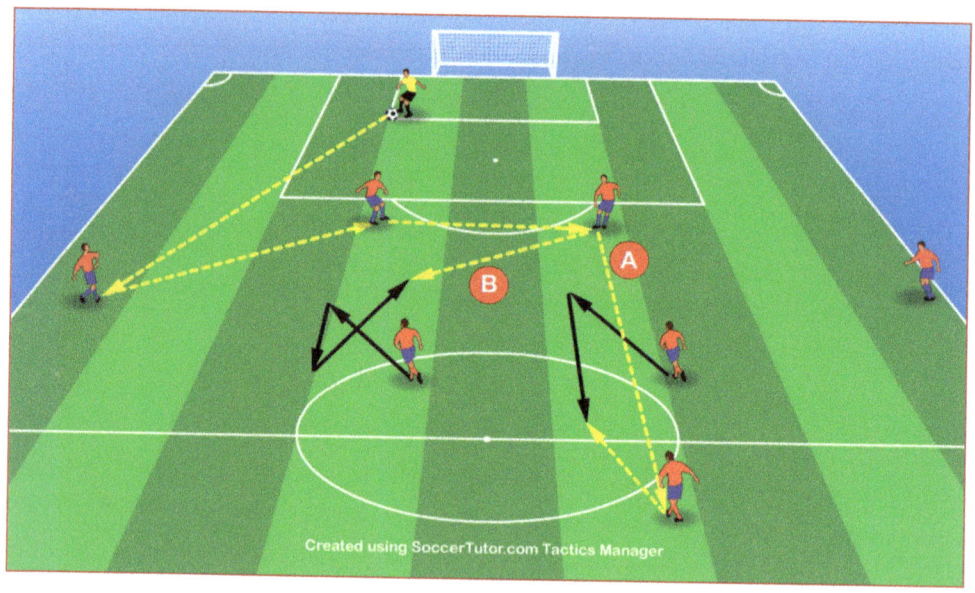

Description (including Coaching Points)

We start this pattern of play again with a short goal kick. The objective remains the same again, to receive the ball facing the opposition goal and with a full field of vision. This time the ball is passed one more time across to the second centre back

After the 2 initial movements by the midfielder nearest to the ball as seen in the previous practices, and in view of the decision taken by the player in possession (defending and circulating the ball), make the players offer a different passing option (option B).

The midfielder furthest away from the ball at the start, after practicing the movement outlined in the previous practice, should make his run to be in line with the most advanced player in his team (as shown in the diagram). Option A is again a pass to the forward with the second centre midfielder moving to receive the pass back.

At least 2 passing options must be available to whichever centre midfielder receives the ball for the practice to be considered a success and when the midfielder receives the ball, he should be facing the opposition's half thus having a better field of vision.

RAFA JUANES Villareal CF Technical Academy Coordinator

Switching Play from One Flank to the Other using the Centre Midfielders

20 min

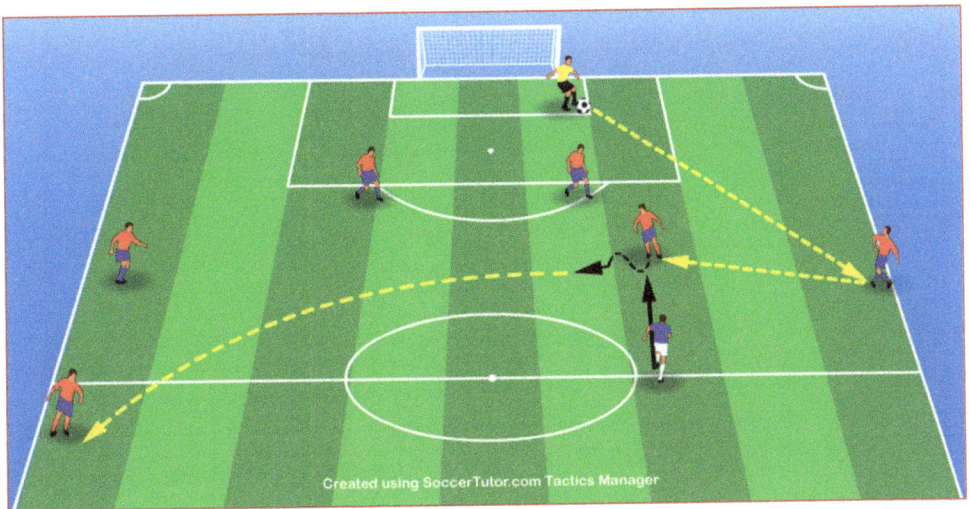

Objective
We work on a tactical situation; building up play after switching the ball out wide.

Description (including Coaching Points)
For this practice we have a goalkeeper, the back 4, 1 centre midfielder and 1 winger. Start again with a short goal kick. There is also 1 opposition midfielder (blue).

The full back receives and passes or passes first time to the centre midfielder. This decision depends on the speed of the ball, distance from the opponent and the amount of pressure.

The ball must be played in the opposite direction to the pressure of the 1 opposition player (blue) in order to make him change direction. This gives the player in possession the time to execute the subsequent action comfortably and correctly. The move ends with a long pass to the winger (switching play) executed with the foot on the side under the least pressure.

Coaching Points
1. It is important to take into account the player's balance when receiving and passing the ball.
2. The entire practice should be carried out with the players facing the opposition's half so the players have a wide field of vision.

RAFA JUANES Villareal CF Technical Academy Coordinator

Switching Play from One Flank to the Other using the Centre Midfielders (2)

20 min

Objective
We work on a tactical situation; building up play after playing the ball out wide.

Description
This is a variation of the previous practice and we add the second centre midfielder.

This time, when the centre midfielder receives, he passes to the other centre midfielder and moves around the opponent in order to receive back in behind him (1-2 combination).

The move ends with a long pass to the winger (switching play) executed with the foot on the side under the least pressure.

Coaching Points
1. It is important for take into account the player's balance, both when receiving and striking the ball (switching the play with a long pass).
2. This entire drill should be carried out with the players facing the opposition's half so the players have a wide field of vision.

RAFA JUANES Villareal CF Technical Academy Coordinator

Controlled Interception from a Goal Kick and Change of Direction to Start an Attack

20 min

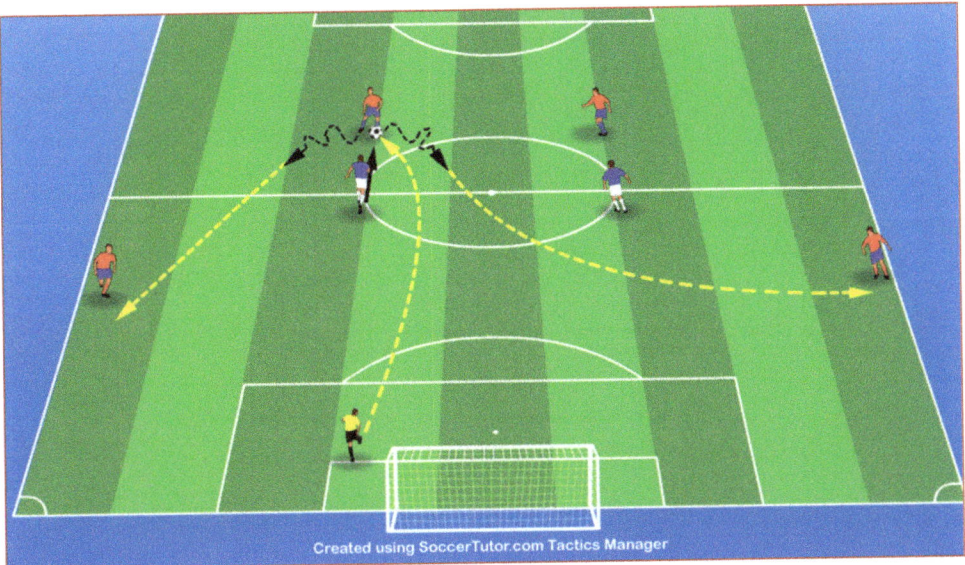

Objective
We work on defending from a goal kick and then passing out wide.

Description
We work with 2 centre backs, 2 wingers and 2 opposition forwards. Start the practice with a goal kick from the opposition goalkeeper. We have 2 centre backs put under pressure by the 2 blue forwards.

One centre back must control the ball and they have 2 wingers that they need to work the ball to in the opposition half. The move ends with a long pass to the winger (2 options shown) executed with the foot on the side under the least pressure.

Coaching Points
1. One centre back needs a controlled interception executed with the part of the body appropriate to the height of the ball.
2. It is important to take into account the player's balance when receiving and passing the ball.
3. The players should always be facing the zone occupied by the attacking team so that the player can modify the angle of their run to make contact with the ball, thus giving them time to perform the subsequent action.

RAFA JUANES Villareal CF Technical Academy Coordinator

Modifying Positioning while Running Backwards & Controlled Headed Clearances to Start an Attack

20 min

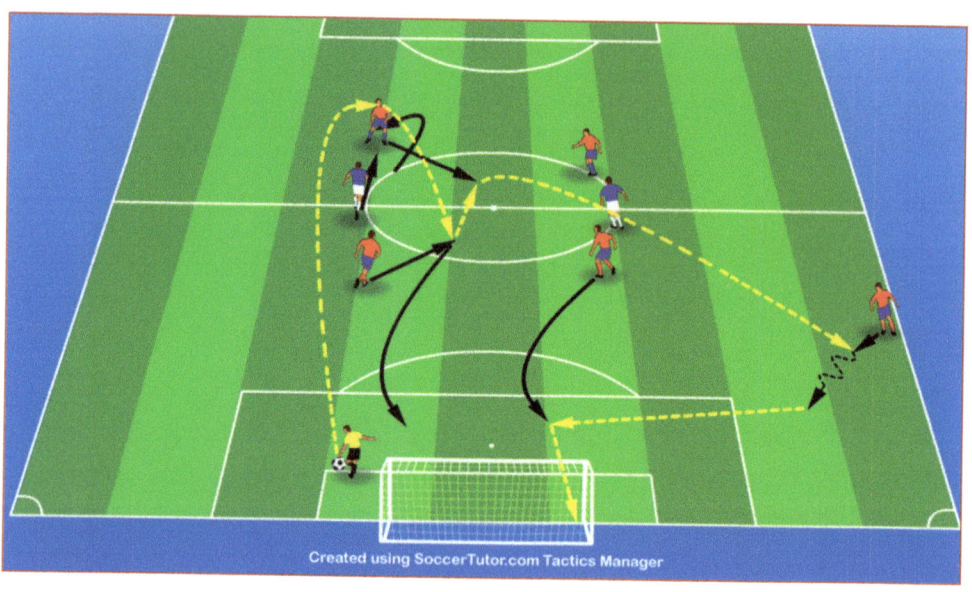

Objective
We work on defending from a goal kick and then moving quickly into the attacking phase.

Description
We now add 2 centre midfielders from the previous practice and start again with a goal kick. The 2 red centre backs must modify their defensive positioning while running backwards and looking to head the ball.

In contrast to the movement of the centre backs when tracking back, the centre midfielders should always move backwards as their task is to reinforce the defence and move forwards to make a clearance. If the ball is played over them, they then collaborate with their defensive teammates behind them.

If the headed clearance is accurate, the team can then move into the attacking phase. The move ends with a 1-2 combination or a long pass to the winger (switching play).

Coaching Points
1. Pay attention to the difference in the heading technique for defenders and midfielders.
2. Once the player is in the correct position to make contact with the ball, they should head the clearance in the direction of a teammate (head through the middle of the ball).
3. The player must always be aware of what is around him and the position of his teammates in order to control the headed clearance and make sure it reaches a teammate.

RAFA JUANES Villareal CF Technical Academy Coordinator

Centre Midfield Combination Play after Defending a Long Ball

20 min

Example 1

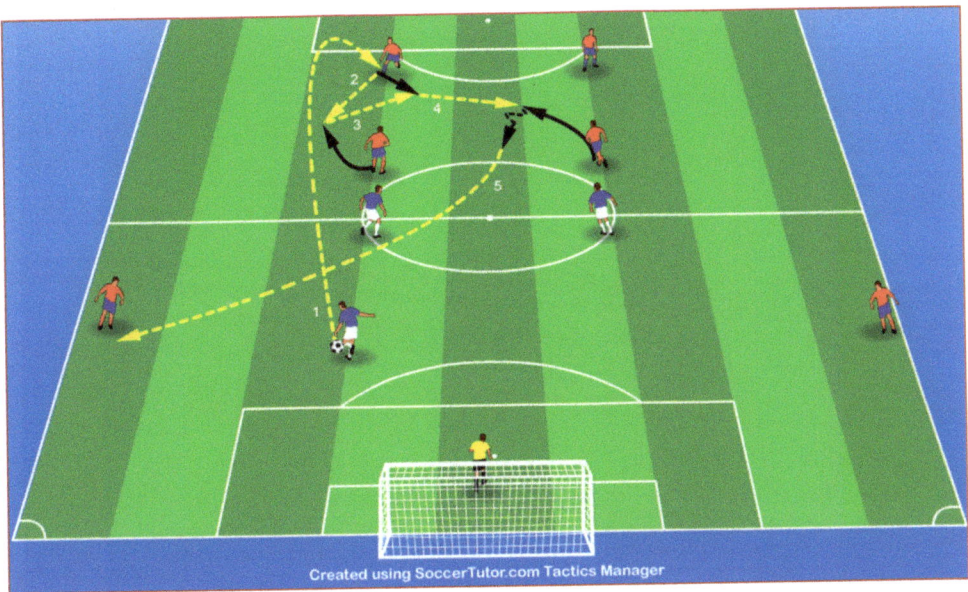

Example 2

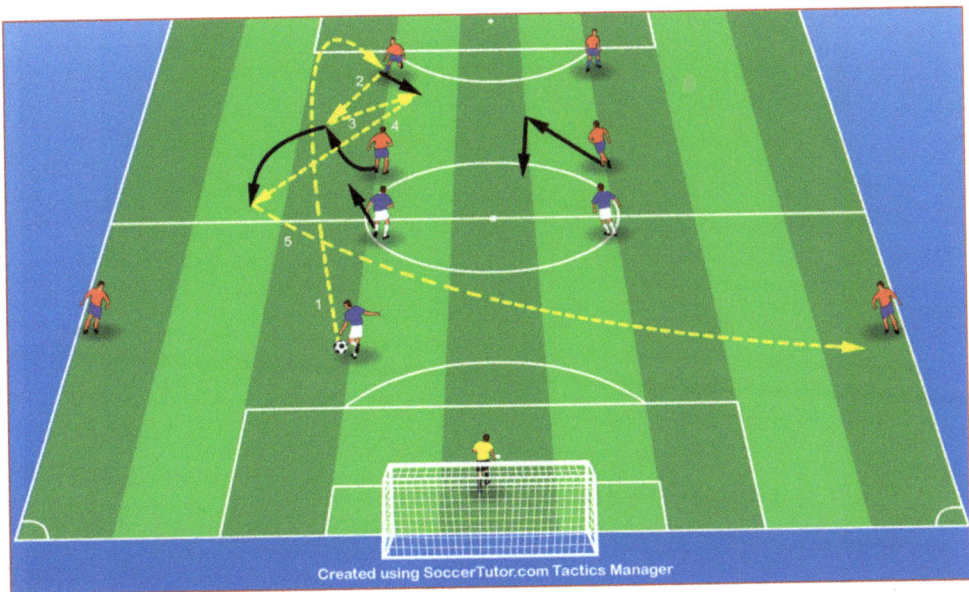

©SoccerTutor.com

Advanced Spanish Academy Coaching

RAFA JUANES Villareal CF Technical Academy Coordinator

Example 3

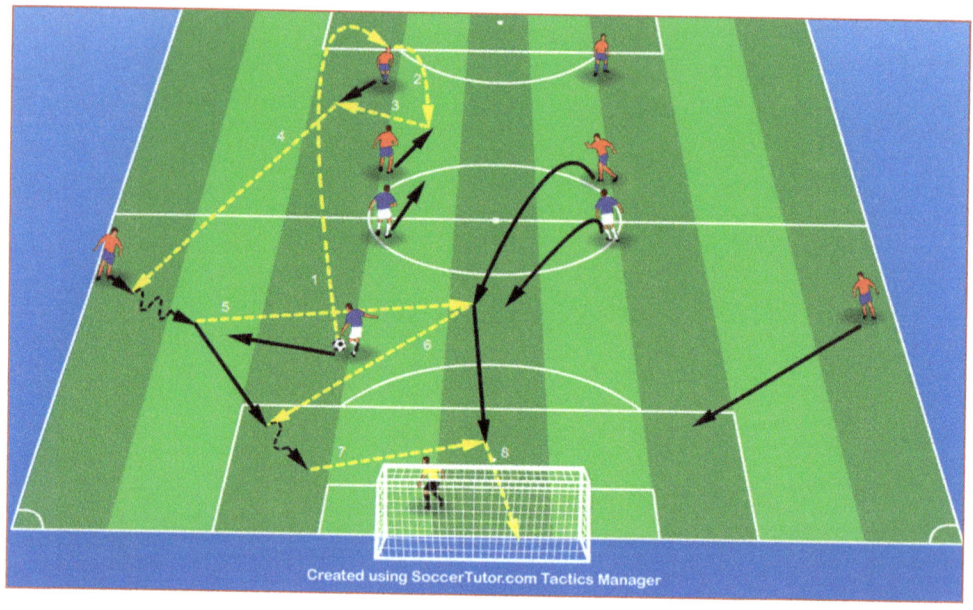

Objective
We work on defending a long ball and building up play (passing & movement between the 2 centre midfielders).

Description
We add 1 more winger and 1 opponent from the previous practice and start again with a long ball from the blue centre back. One red centre back should control the ball and play a short pass to start an attacking move.

Once he has played the pass, 1 centre midfielder should move to make himself available for the return, always aware of the position of the other centre midfielder so the player in possession always has 2 passing options.

3 examples of attacks have been shown in the diagrams with the 2 centre midfielders playing a pivotal role in each.

Coaching Points
1. It is important to emphasise that this practice is focused on passing and movement in pairs between the 2 centre midfielders and the centre back who receives.
2. The players need to be ready in the centre to receive the ball as it is cleared.

RAFA JUANES Villareal CF Technical Academy Coordinator

SPECIAL PROGRAM TO DEVELOP TECHNICAL PERFECTION THROUGH TACTICAL POSITIONING: FORWARDS

Program Development

In this last section, we look at the development of technical training specifically for **forwards**.

When looking at and evaluating the different practices we have to take into account the skills outlined in the following diagram.

Depending on the generic method already used, the actions that we must develop and improve are as follows:

PASSES	1. Short pass, movement & individual actions. 2. Passing and shooting on the run.
CONTROL	1. Close control and shooting. 2. Control after a feint. 3. Cushioning and team actions.
INDIVIDUAL ACTIONS	1. Shooting. 2. Dummy shot with limited number of touches. 3. Shooting from a static position. 4. Shooting and dribbling without visual perception. 5. Covering and movement.
DEFENSIVE HEADING	1. Static lateral headers. 2. Lateral headers with a short run up.
ATTACKING HEADING	1. Lateral headers with a short run up. 2. Attacking headers. 3. Flick ons.
TECHNICAL ACTIONS	1. Profile. 2. Timing.

PRACTICAL APPLICATION

When developing and evaluating the execution of the different exercises we have to take the following into account:

SPECIFIC ELEMENTS	CONDITIONS
Spatial orientation	As similar as possible to reality
Physical imbalances	Situational analysis (from part to the whole)
Protection and physical opposition	Use real actions
Dominant leg	Strong and real opposition
Reading of tactical references	Evaluate temporal and spatial orientation
Decision making	Precise application to the game, not just learning through drills
Mechanisation of technical movements	

RAFA JUANES Villareal CF Technical Academy Coordinator

Collective and Coordinated Movements of the Front 6 With & Without the Ball

20 min

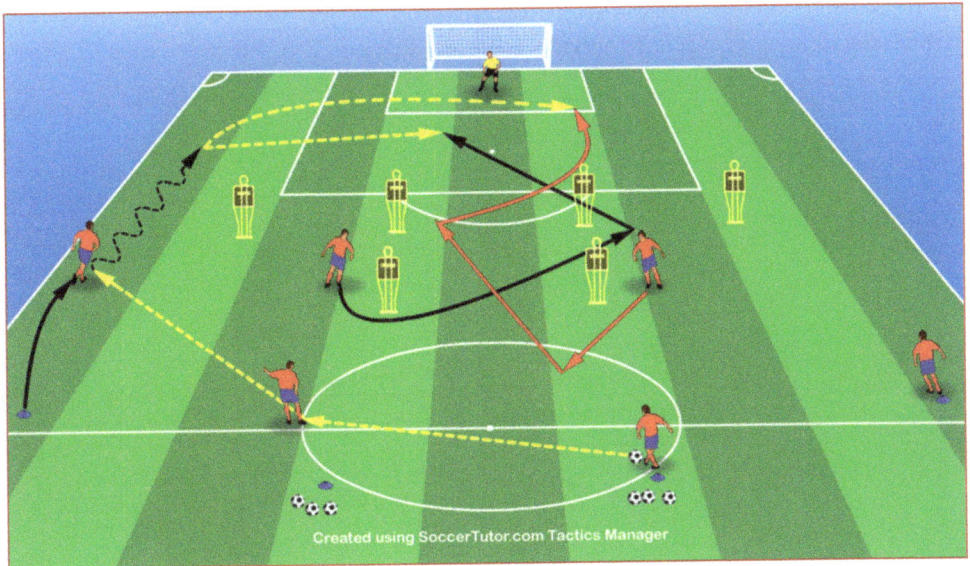

Objective
We work on a tactical situation, focusing on coordinating the movement of the forwards/midfield according to the position of the ball and the opposition defenders.

Description
We play with the front 6 and mannequins to show the positions of the opposition. For the first part of the exercise we work on the coordinated support of the forwards and midfielders who collectively close down the opponents (mannequins) in a semi circle across the pitch.

We then pretend possession is gained and 1 centre midfielder plays a ball out wide and the forwards alter both their intent and positioning. The second part of the exercise looks at the positioning of the forward and how he looks for alternatives after the ball is played wide.

During this phase, the aforementioned semi circle is inversed, offering 2 options to the player in possession of the ball:

1. Allowing the ball to be played in diagonally to the near post.
2. A one-two combination with one of the supporting midfielders to then cross to the far post.

The exercise ends when one of the forwards takes a shot at goal. Their movement is shown by the black/red arrows as they try to escape the opposition and score.

RAFA JUANES Villareal CF Technical Academy Coordinator

Collective and Coordinated Movements of the Front 6 With & Without the Ball (2)

20 min

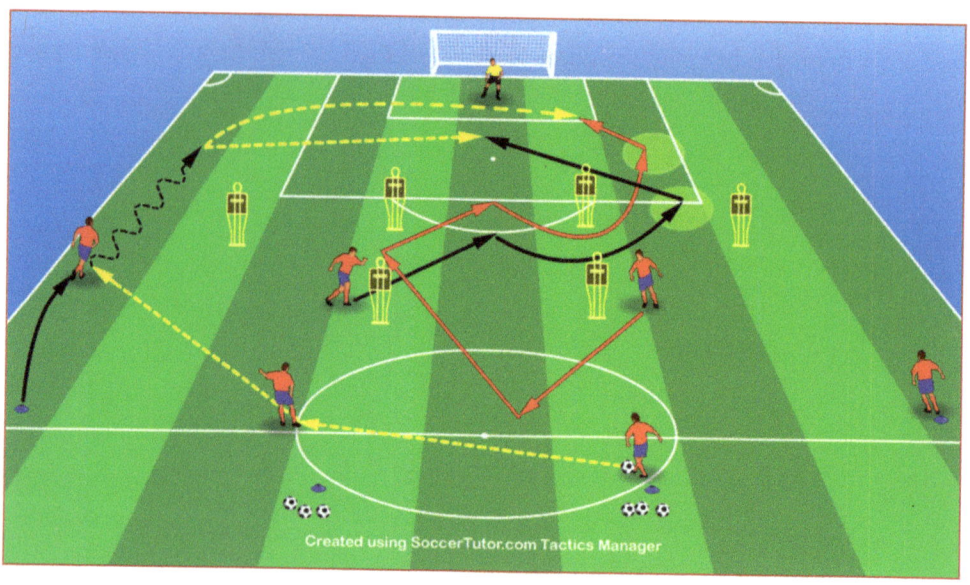

Objective
We work on a tactical situation, focusing on coordinating the movement of the forwards according to the position of the ball and the opposition defenders.

Description
This is a variation of the previous practice with one difference. The forwards must now modify their movements and look for immediate and alternative answers.

We observe how, in the movements indicated by the highlighted 'waiting areas' in the diagram, 2 different consecutive actions are produced. They unite a diagonal and a curved movement into the same action.

The forwards can assume either of these positions depending on whether the player in possession chooses to delay his pass or in order to avoid being played offside by the defence.

As with the previous practice, the player in possession should have 2 options where to play the ball.

RAFA JUANES Villareal CF Technical Academy Coordinator

Coordinated Movements for Attacking on the Flanks with Crossing & Finishing

20 min

A

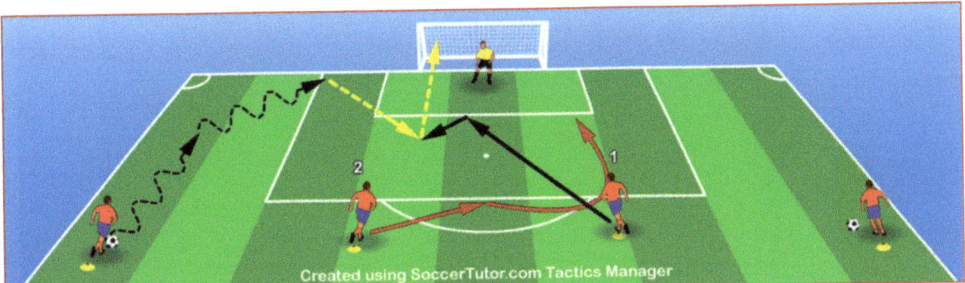

B

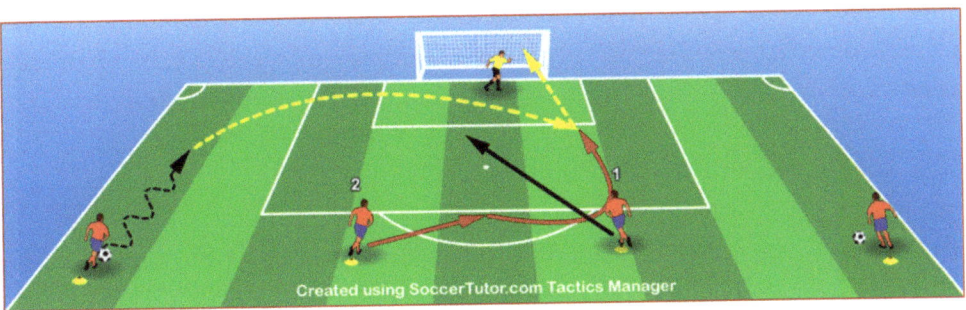

Objective
We work on a tactical situation, focusing on the movement of the forwards towards the 2 points inside the penalty area where a wide player will cross the ball.

Description (including Coaching Points)
The wide player starts with the ball and dribbles forward alongside the penalty area. Before the player in possession on the wing crosses the ball, the forwards must coordinate their movements so that the winger has 2 options of where to cross the ball.

Player 1 makes a diagonal run into the centre of the box and then makes a movement backwards to receive the short cross at the near post. Player 2 makes a short diagonal run to the edge of the area, followed by a curved run towards the far post, keeping his head up and facing the ball, ready for the player in possession to play a deep cross to the far post.

The exercise ends with a one touch effort on goal with whichever part of the body is most appropriate depending on the height of the cross.

©SoccerTutor.com *Advanced Spanish Academy Coaching*

Coordinated Movements for Attacking on the Flanks with Crossing & Finishing (2)

20 min

Objective
We work on a tactical situation, focusing on the movements of the 2 forwards when a teammate is attacking down the wing against strong opposition.

Description
Here we have a progression to the previous practice and add a defender out wide. The wide player must resist the defender (who starts from the position shown) in order to put the cross in.

The forwards must support the wide player by moving into good positions and making themselves available for a pass/cross while taking the entire situation into account.

Both forwards should be prepared for a pass to the near post because if the winger is under considerable pressure, a pass/cross to the far post is much more unlikely to be possible.

Player 1 makes a direct diagonal run across the area looking to make himself available for the pass which will usually come along the goal line and around the defender.

Player 2 makes a small movement towards the penalty spot in an attempt to create space that allows him to adjust his own movement and escape his marker to get to the near post.

RAFA JUANES Villareal CF Technical Academy Coordinator

Movement of the Forwards: Diagonal Runs to Escape a Marker

20 min

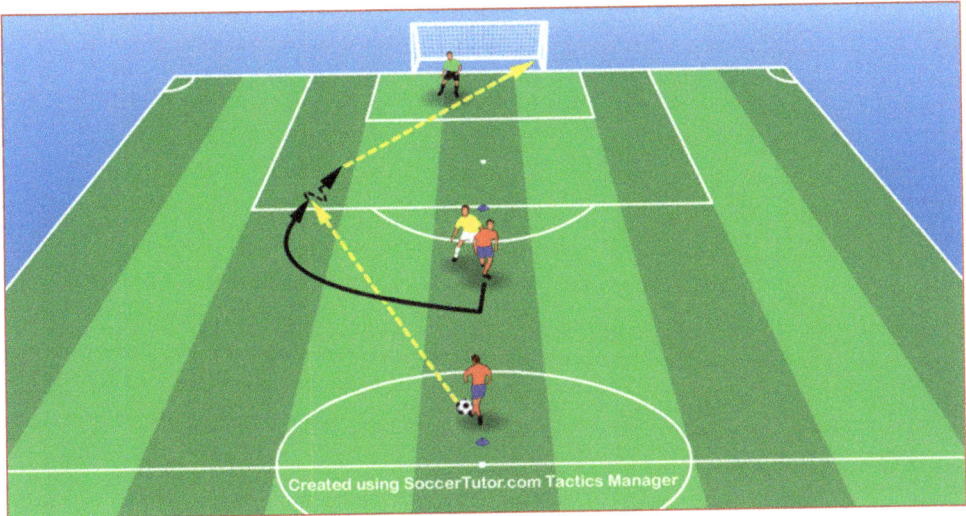

Objective
We work on a technical/tactical situation, focusing on forwards creating space for themselves to then run into.

Description
We work with 2 forwards here against 1 defender.

One forward starts in a deep position and passes to one side of his teammate. That player checks away from their marker, turns and makes a diagonal sprint into the empty space to receive the pass.

The practice concludes with a shot on goal (using either 1 or 2 touches). Both of these actions must be executed with the leg on the side under the least pressure.

Coaching Point
When turning his body, the player should keep his head turned towards the ball so that he is aware of its position and can immediately collect the pass from his teammate and be facing the goal.

RAFA JUANES Villareal CF Technical Academy Coordinator

Forward Play: Receiving with Back to Goal, Protecting the Ball and Finishing

20 min

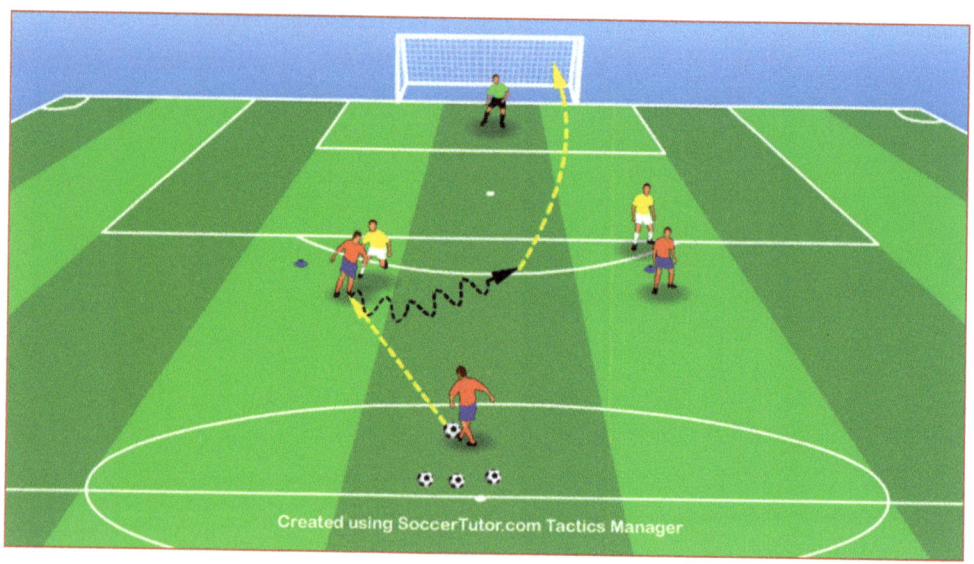

Objective
To develop the correct body shape to protect the ball, get around an opponent and finish.

Description
During a game a forward will often receive the ball with his back to goal, close to the defence in positions around the edge of the area with no easy pass to a teammate available.

We work with 2 players against 1 defender. The forward receives the ball from his teammate with his back to goal and with pressure applied behind him from a defender. The forward should have his arm out to hold off the defender.

After making contact with the defender, the player should turn in the direction his arm was indicating without losing contact with the opposing players body and position his body between the defender and the ball. The practice ends with a shot on goal.

Coaching Points
1. The players arm should be in contact with the defenders body so that he knows where he is at all times and to keep a little distance between the defender and the ball.
2. If the arm is used correctly it will help the player to play the ball, turn and get in a position to take a shot without the defender getting close enough to intercept.

RAFA JUANES Villareal CF Technical Academy Coordinator

Technical: Shooting on the Run from a Tight Angle   20 min

Objective
To develop shooting on the run at an angle to the goal.

Description
Here we work with 2 players and a goalkeeper. We work on a simple action aimed at improving the quality of shots taken whilst on the run.

The player makes a diagonal run to meet his teammates pass on the run and takes a first time shot while at an angle to the goal. We also practice as if under extreme pressure, and can take a touch as if to move the ball away from a defender and take a shot (as shown in the diagram).

Progression: Add a defender to make the practice opposed and more game realistic.

Coaching Points
1. Emphasise the need for the shot to be taken by the most appropriate foot, not necessarily the foot the player is most comfortable.
2. The player must adapt the speed of their run to the pass, in order to strike the ball as cleanly as possible.

RAFA JUANES Villareal CF Technical Academy Coordinator

Diagonal Run, Quick Change of Direction and Finishing using Both Feet

20 min

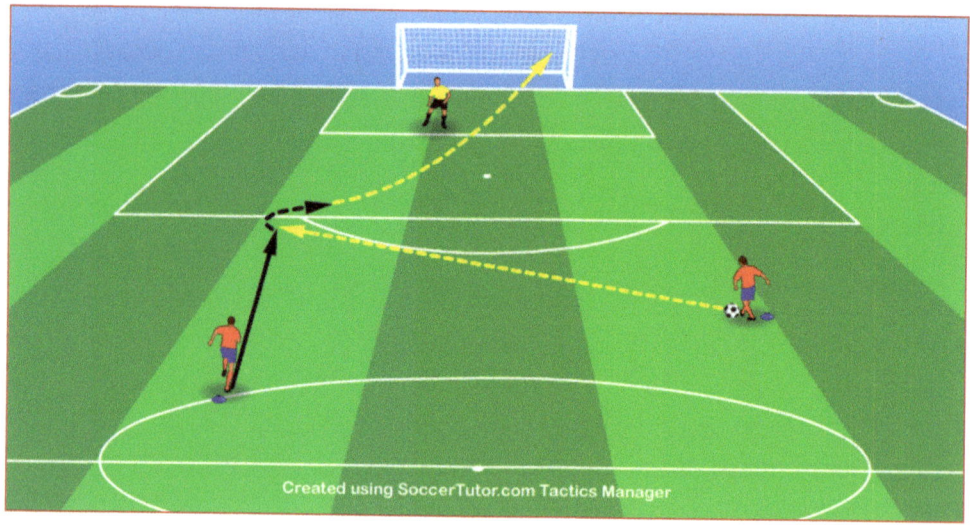

Objective
To develop receiving on the run, changing direction and shooting at an angle to the goal.

Description
This is a variation of the previous drill.

The player runs inside with the ball after receiving this time, quickly changing direction to take a shot with the opposite foot (this should be done as if under pressure from a defender).

Progression: Add a defender to make the practice opposed and more game realistic.

Coaching Points

1. It is important to take into account the mechanisation of the process of slowing down and changing direction so that the player can change direction more quickly.

2. When the player slows down to change direction, he must lower his centre of gravity, taking his weight on the leg that is not taking the shot so that he keeps his balance and can get maximum power behind the shot.

RAFA JUANES Villareal CF Technical Academy Coordinator

Diagonal Run Across the Penalty Area and Finishing Against the Direction of the Run

20 min

Objective
We work on finishing in the opposite direction to the direction of the run with 1 touch.

Description
We again work with 2 players and a goalkeeper. This practice develops the ability to finish first time while on the run, generally using their weaker foot as it is the most difficult movement to coordinate. The player must control the contact with their weaker foot while on the turn.

This practice is very simple in its execution as we have 1 player out wide crossing into the box. The forward makes a diagonal run towards the post nearest to the ball and reaches the ball at an angle to the goal. The shot must be taken with the foot furthest from the goal, using the instep. You can also practice using the top of the foot.

Progression: Add a passive defender who puts the forward under pressure.

Coaching Points
1. It is important to pay attention to the positioning of the supporting leg to allow for the twisting of that leg that will make contact with the ball.
2. Make sure that the players use their arms to balance themselves when taking the shot.

Diagonal Run Across the Penalty Area, Receive with Back to Goal, Turn and Shoot

20 min

Objective
We work on receiving the ball in the penalty area after a diagonal run where it is not possible to shoot immediately.

Description
This is a variation of the previous practice. The player receives the ball and is unable to take an immediate shot due to either the proximity of a defender or the location of the ball, so must look for alternative options.

The player must control the ball with his back to the goal, keeping his body between the defender (can use a cone or mannequin) and the ball. The player must then turn and shoot.

Progression: Add a passive defender who puts the forward under pressure.

Coaching Point
An important part of this drill is physicality. The player must use his body to shield the ball, using the method fully explained on page 87.

CHAPTER 3

MANU DORADO

Real Madrid Academy Coach and former Malaga CF Coach

REAL MADRID ACADEMY COACH PROFILE

Manu Dorado
Real Madrid Academy Coach

Previous Coaching positions:
- Malaga CF Academy Coach

Credentials:
- UEFA A Licence
- National Coach Bachelor of Physical preparation
- Technical Sports Degree

CONCEPTS FOR TRAINING: LEARNING TO DEAL WITH SPECIFIC SITUATIONS

Specific learning concepts used as tools to create intelligent players:
Whenever I see a coach on the touchline in their technical area, shouting himself hoarse, throwing instructions left and right to his players, I think the same thing, 'all of this is because his players have not fully understood and developed all of the concepts that their coach has tried to teach them'.

Immediately afterwards I try to learn a little more about the team and the players (looking at the individual, team and group behaviour during the next few games) and also try to learn a little more about the coach, enquiring about his methodology.

I do this to try to figure out if the initial problems I was talking about are due to an 'improved capacity' to absorb the information and subsequent application on behalf of the players during the game or if it is the opposite, an 'incomplete methodology of learning' on behalf of the coach.

I say 'incomplete' because there are occasions when it is evident in games that players still rely on their coaches to help complete their actions. I think the the best way to get your team to play well every week is to transfer the autonomous and independent concepts, procedures and attitudes worked on daily in training into a competitive game.

Coaches have a tendency to think that it is enough to train the players in an aspect of the game without spending sufficient time to evaluate and to verify that the information has been understood fully by the players.

There have been many times when we we have all been surprised to see that our players have really not taken in what we intended to convey in a game.

This is why, in this chapter we are going to try to kill 2 birds with 1 stone.

On one side we will look at a type of training that is not currently used much: 'concept specific training'.

On the other side we have a methodology that many coaches talk about, but that you rarely see in training. This is a guided discovery through questions or problematic situations, where the players must solve the difficulties themselves or answer questions that the coach will pose.

They therefore try to make the learning significant, so that the concepts are learned and the players do not always depend on their coaches.

Manu Dorado Real Madrid Academy Coach

WHY IS IT IMPORTANT TO LEARN THROUGH CONCEPTS?

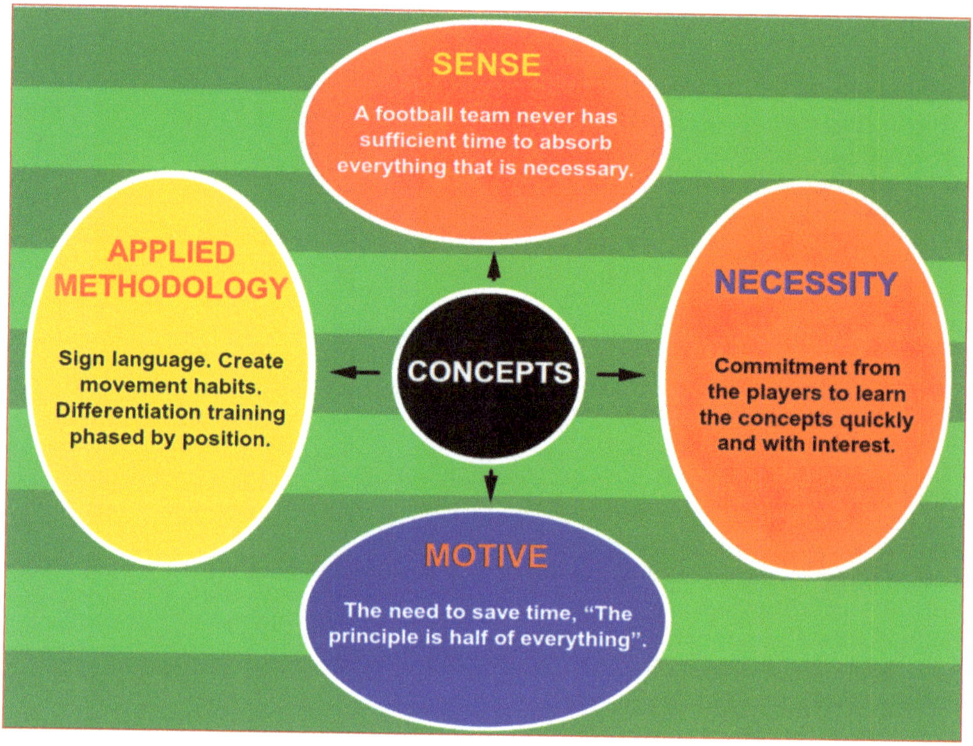

SENSE
A football team never has sufficient time to absorb everything that is necessary.

APPLIED METHODOLOGY
Sign language. Create movement habits. Differentiation training phased by position.

CONCEPTS

NECESSITY
Commitment from the players to learn the concepts quickly and with interest.

MOTIVE
The need to save time, "The principle is half of everything".

It is all very well to dominate and manage the concepts of the game (most of us know football, or rather, we think we know), but it is quite another thing to master the skills needed to apply these concepts appropriately during a game. As Juan Manuel Lillo says, a coach should get players to learn the concepts and find out the solutions without having to say them directly, through learning in games and training exercises.

In recent years progress has been made in the approach to a global methodology that is more specific to our sport, but we still have much to do to improve and achieve what should be the main objective of any coach; to teach and not merely explain.

This helps us train our players in football instead of athleticism (to cite one training method widely used a few years ago). If we do not know why we are doing it, what is better or worse and how do we know if we are doing it well?

Manu Dorado Real Madrid Academy Coach

These days, with the resources available on the Internet, any sports coach can build a global training method "copying" the tasks found on many websites and can use some of them with his players, but from doing that to actually extracting the essence of each of the concepts, their specifics and the useful learning of said concepts, takes a willingness to learn on behalf of both the coach and the players.

When we talk about specific training workouts we talk about training based on a specific sport. In football, training is based on the stimuli of competition where players solve problems either individually, in groups or collectively, which are similar to those of the competition.

When we say 'similar' we are thinking about the physical, technical, tactical, psychological and decision making challenges and must keep all of the context as real as possible. Francisco Seirul'lo said while referring to training, that players should practice 'within the specific environmental elements' of football.

As we can all draw from the above, one aspect that takes a special role is the cognitive aspect, as intelligence is necessary in order to reach the ultimate goal in any training.

Players minds need to be on the game, ready to tackle and solve problems and not, as happens too often, to act as mere puppets or robots looking to obey any order from their coach.

What place do the coaches have in all of this?

Although in this sport the real protagonists are the players and not us, it still seems logical to think that our place is very important (secondary but fundamental at the same time).

To study each game situation in minute-by-minute detail, to look at specific situations or prepare the players to face each problem or unforeseen situation during a game can really help the players learn and make the correct decisions on the pitch.

'DO NOT TRY TO GIVE FISH TO OUR PLAYERS, BUT TEACH THEM HOW TO FISH.'

CONCEPTS OF THE GAME

The principals that should help us understand the tactical learning of our players is the ADVANCEMENT towards learning effectiveness, both individually and collectively, of the concepts that govern our sport.

There are many books that give us magical methods for training, for each session, each category, each level, each country etc, but where is the evolution of the concepts?

And above all, where are the characteristics of our team? From the peculiarities that each team possesses, that each coach wants, come the priorities.

The concepts of the game are not entirely universal in their application; the following is an example of prioritisation of concepts in 2 phases (ATTACK & DEFENCE):

Attacking Phase

1. Basic concepts
2. Tasks by position and communication/body language
3. Original positions and attacking movement
4. Tactical individual positions
5. Movement of the ball
6. Transition from defence to attack with recovery in the first line
7. Transition from defence to attack after winning the ball in the second or third line
8. Direct attack
9. Combining attacks down the wings
10. Group play down the wings
11. How to avoid being in offside positions
12. Counter Attacking: Defence going forward, in central, backwards or closed positions
13. Counter Attacking: Superior, equal or inferior in numbers
14. Attacking balance
15. Overcoming pressing
16. Dead Ball Situations: Corners
17. Dead Ball Situations: Indirect free kicks
18. Dead Ball Situations: Throw-ins
19. Dead Ball Situations: Centres / Kick-off
20. Others

Manu Dorado Real Madrid Academy Coach

Defensive Phase

1. Basic concepts
2. Positional Tasks: Defensive positioning
3. Original positioning and defensive movement
4. Transition from attack to defence - retreating
5. Transition from attack to defence if the defenders were forward
6. Transition from attack to defence if the ball is lost in midfield
7. Transition from attack to defence if the ball is lost down the wings
8. Retreating before the transition from attack to defence
9. Positioning for frontal attacks
10. Positioning for lateral attacks (behind the first line)
11. Positioning for lateral attacks (behind the second line)
12. Pressuring in various situations
13. Advanced positional pressuring
14. Team pressuring
15. With the ball between the first and second line
16. Defending the ball with your back to goal
17. Clearances and getting the ball off the line
18. Playing offside
19. Defending your goalkeeper when outnumbered
20. Defending against superiority and equality in numbers and when outnumbered
21. Defending against attacks from the wings
22. Positioning when defending a corner
23. Positioning when defending indirect free kicks
24. Others

For all of these game concepts you can establish the following work related content:

CONTENT TO WORK ON		
Exercises to create and occupy free space	Game of "Playing the ball backwards"	Possession of the ball
Attacking dead ball exercises	Team divided into groups	Games on half the pitch, limited or unlimited number of touches
Exercises for numerical inferiority	Defensive dead ball exercises	Organisation of attacking play, blocking midfielders and forwards, defending with a goal
Tactical exercises in pressing	Exercises in playing players offside	Double area
Exercises in wing play	A game to ensure the defensive and attacking organisation	Combining actions with various objectives e.g. pressing and finishing
Game with 4 or 6 goals	Game with specific exercises such as assists or through balls	Game on a smaller pitch with small goals

In addition to all the concepts that we can find to work systematically and individually with our players, the coach must recognise how to neutralise the potential game situations resulting from these concepts. In the following table, tactical solutions arise from game concepts.

Losing your marker	Zonal marking, tracking back, pressing your marker, offside tactics
Counter attacks	Pressing the ball, tracking back, playing a defensive line, offside tactics
Attacks	Covering, depth and breadth of defence, timing
Overlapping	Tracking back, zonal marking, pressing
Vigilance	Constant movement
Open spaces	Tracking back and zonal marking
Support and help	Total pressure on support players, tracking back
Walls	Good coverage, zonal marking, pressing, anticipation
Controlling the game with possession	Total pressure with half the pitch in front of you
Collective change of pace	Tracking back, zonal marking
Individual change of pace	Pressing and keeping the ball
Changes of directions	Zonal marking, tracking back, defensive lines, pressing the ball, anticipation
Speed and progression	Zonal marking, switching markers, covering and swapping positions
Timings	Covering, pressuring the ball

Once we have established the game concepts and organised them by phases we get to the meaningful learning. That is, the situations in which we will see each concept and especially what problems will arise for the player when integrated into the game itself.

The player should know how to answer these questions in the Attacking Phase:

- When I have the ball, how do I perform individually? And what if a teammate has the ball?
- When I have the ball, how do we perform as a group? And what if a teammate has the ball?
- When I have the ball, what can I do to help my team?
- How do I act in a dead ball situation?
- What 3 things should we be doing to regain possession of the ball?
- In what 3 ways can we attack?
- When we play, what is our system? What are our three phases?

The secret is in the design of the tasks. We must look further than a tactical, technical or physical concept. We must move from general to specific and we must move from global knowledge to individual knowledge.

Global Task - 3 v 2 Possession Exercise

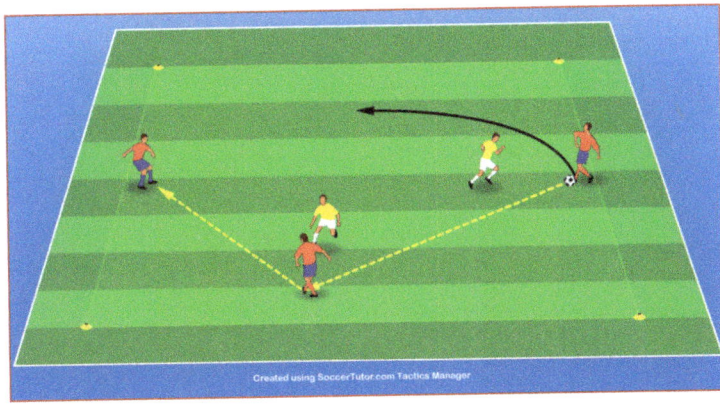

Objective
To develop passing, awareness of space, maintaining possession and player movement.

Description
We play 3 against 2 within a predetermined area with no criteria to follow so we are making a comprehensive collective activity, putting into action all of the in-game factors.

Coaching Point
Create passing lanes, protect the ball, control/pass quickly and use collective pressing.

Manu Dorado Real Madrid Academy Coach

Collective Structured Task - Introduction to Direction of Play in a 3v2 Dynamic Small Sided Game

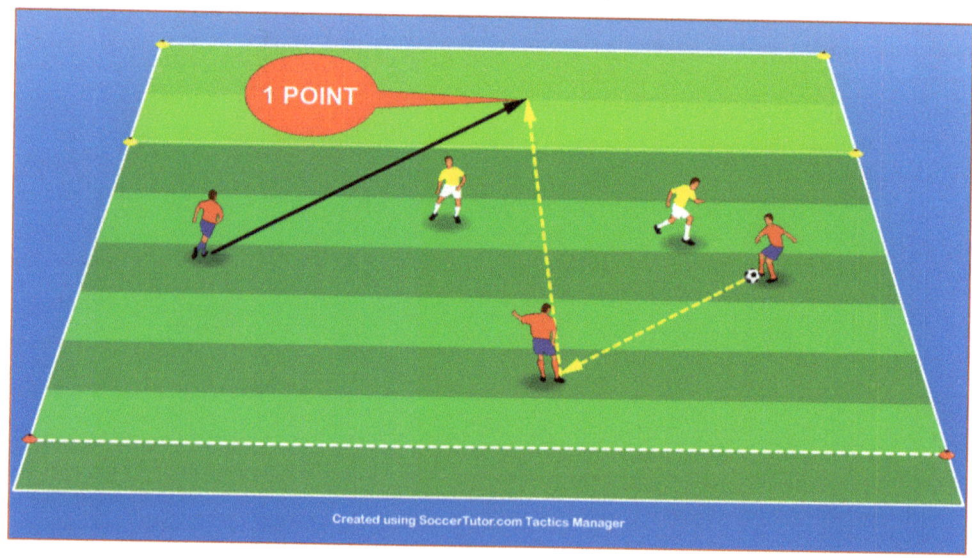

Objective
We still develop passing, awareness of space, maintaining possession and player movement, but now progress to work on collective tasks such as attacking in one direction and zonal defending.

Description
In this 3v2 progression we introduce the direction of play. The reds attack the yellows (a sense of progression) and the defenders have the zone to defend (a sense of protection).

One red player must pass to another inside the end zone who control the ball within it to score a point. If the yellows intercept/win the ball, they dribble through the end line at the opposite end to score a point.

Progression: Apply the offside rule throughout the practice.

Coaching Points
1. Beware that simply adding the collective tasks may be insufficient because it generally ends in anarchy and individualism, or, in a word, disorder.
2. The players should focus on zonal defending, collective pressing, protecting the ball and zone, where and when to attack etc.

SPECIFIC LEARNING CONCEPTS AS A TOOL FOR CREATING INTELLIGENT PLAYERS

If, as coaches, we can get our players to be "thinking players" during our training sessions through "problematic" tasks or situations we will walk the path that leads us to the ultimate goal, that is, to "build" players who are intelligent and autonomous during competition. They will be independent of the control of the coaches.

Earlier, when we said that the players are the real stars of the sport, we also made reference to the prominence it gives them to be the ones ultimately responsible for the technical/tactical decisions made during a game.

We, as the ones responsible for training the players, have to present them with problems and guide them towards a solution, but ultimately it is the players who must solve it and not us.

So of course, render unto Caesar the things which are Caesar's, the richer the content that we introduce to the training sessions the sooner we may arrive at our goal, that they learn to interpret all of the stimuli and principles that develop during a game, adapting to the continuous changes (if there are any) and controlling and choosing the appropriate response at that time.

We try to implement all of this during the training sessions to guide players to the correct positions and through the discovery propose parts of a question. From this, through the options we propose to the players, they have the option to extend their experiences first (regardless of the time they need in order to discover the correct answer).

Once the best solution is discovered for this particular problem and is defined as "correct" by all members of the team (both coaches and players) the problem can be "closed" (if there is nothing similar). So it seems logical to guess that the player will be the true protagonist of their own learning process on the road towards autonomy.

Jose Mourinho says that one of the main objectives he has with his players is to ensure that when they step out onto the pitch they know exactly what to do and how to do it, training what it is they need to do on the day, so they can go out and do it.

To ensure that they not only reach this objective but that their assimilation is long term, they must convert their learning into behavioural patterns.

We propose a methodology based on a type of guided discovery where we talk, ask for their feelings or let them take the lead when they provide interesting answers to the questions laid out (and from there it becomes a habit).

Manu Dorado Real Madrid Academy Coach

If you were to ask an experienced winger what he would usually do when an opposing player (his direct opponent on the wing, for example) dribbles the ball towards him with the intention of going around him, we would possibly find a common answer.

So often we arrive at (if it has not been left behind long ago) the traditional learning model, although in these cases we rely only on experience and this does not guarantee much, and does not guarantee what we seek: INTELLIGENT PLAYERS.

What if we have been doing things wrong for a long time?

Our methodological approach goes a little further, asking the player in this case:

Why do you do this and not that?
Have you ever considered other options?

We understand that if we reason through what we do and the reasons why we do it, we can try different options to expand the possibilities of a different response and therefore the chances of eventual success.

I try different options, comparing the benefits and drawbacks, then we decide (my coach and I) which is the most appropriate and try to make it a habit. Then we are able to move onto the next problem.

Manu Dorado Real Madrid Academy Coach

Collective Movement to Defend the Area in a 6 v 4 Situation

Objective
We aim to put the concepts learnt into practice and work on collective defending and positioning when the ball is moved around.

Description
Here we work with 6 players in possession who simply pass the ball around between themselves, constantly switching the play. There are in a 2-4 or 4-2 formation. The defending team is just a back 4 and they have to move collectively in relation to where the ball is.

The aim is to put the concepts they have learned into practice. In the diagram example, the defenders move forward initially (1st movement), then back and towards the sideline when the reds switch the play (2nd movement).

Coaching Points
In this type of task we can find several variations for a specific job. The tactical situations that arise from the attacking and defending aspects are integrated into the real game. Such tasks should be the end of a long process of learning through concepts and specific tasks.

If we consult with our players and they are convinced (not "we convince them") that our approach is correct, we will have achieved 2 objectives related to their learning as players and our credibility as coaches.

We are also open to change and possible improvements so we will learn much more about how our players think and what they can provide us. The first thing that we as coaches have to be clear about is the concepts that occur during the game, both offensively and defensively.

METHODOLOGY BASED ON GUIDED DISCOVERY THROUGH QUESTIONS

Examples of Specific Practices which are Intended to Incorporate Different Aspects of the Game

These practices aim to show our players that our proposals are usually successful in competition but without imposing them. We instead encourage them to be themselves and they discover what we want from them, although we give them clues. We propose, experiment, talk and discuss the tasks and draw conclusions which all helps to create habits.

Many times coaches find that after explaining and demonstrating something several times for a week during training, that later during a competitive game we see that the players fail to execute as expected. We believed that the explanation had been perfect and the demonstration excellent, yet the astonished faces of our players show that something went wrong.

To avoid this we propose a method that (although it seems slower) is more reliable than other more traditional methods. The method we use is a guided discovery through the question and survey method.

This frees us from some pressure during competitive matches (or allows you to know that your players have mastered the concepts), and you see that the learning itself was significant and that our players solve problems independently and effectively.

Using this type of method means committing to player participation, where instead of telling them what to do and providing the solutions, we give them the option to control the situation themselves.

We all know that all change takes time, and initially they find it difficult to ask the coach questions and make their case in front of their teammates (because of fear of failure or ridicule in front of them). It is therefore of vital importance to reward those who answer, somehow directing their answers to the area we are interested in, until they see this approach of questions and answers as logical and habitual during workouts.

In the same way, in time we will learn to analyse situations, questions and answers. When we are planning the training we can classify the practices to help us put each problem into context and it will give us a clearer way to properly select the specific tasks.

Different Training Methods for Different Circumstances

The Time of Year

1. **Pre-season:** During this stage of the season, getting the players to absorb the training of specific tasks or concepts is the main objective. This can be from the most basic concepts in function and style or form of play based on the system itself.

2. **Competition:** The matches themselves will tell us which aspects of the game must be worked on. This makes the practices more specific and important errors will be detected in the players learning of concepts.

The Number of Players

During the matches I analyse my team and may detect individual, group or team errors. Therefore, during the next week I might be interested in working to correct those individual, group or team errors.

1. **Individual**

2. **Group**

   A) Small drills for 2 players (e.g. on the flank with the midfielder close).
   B) In lines (e.g. a defensive line of 4) and/or in lines (players on the flank).

3. **The Whole Team**

The Phase of the Game
(or more specifically, the sub-phase which you want to work on)

1. **Attack**
2. **Defence**
3. **Transition from Attack to Defence**
4. **Transition from Defence to Attack**

Based on this classification, the range of possible aspects of the game that would fit within what we call the learning concepts through specific training is extensive and if we go by the errors that are detected weekly in professional players, we would cover important concepts that have not been worked on enough such as defensive orientation, communication or peripheral vision.

Practices Based on Real Game Situations and Specific Positions

Next we will show some possible problems based on real situations in a real game, where, with a very basic and simple (with few questions) aim for our players to discover and take in the concepts, making their own conclusions and thereby facilitating learning.

To help their understanding, in each approach and within each type of classification we keep notes as to which aspect we are referring, that is:

1. Depending on the time of year if it would be a good practice for pre-season, during the season or for both.

2. Depending on the number of players if we deal with individuals, groups or team tasks.

3. Depending on which phase of the game we want to work on.

If we want to work on specific positions, such as during the attacking phase, the specific training should be directed towards specific practices where our players try to solve questions such as:

- **Wingers**: How do we lose our markers? When do we cross the ball?

- **Midfielders**: Which zone of the pitch should we be in?

- **Forwards**: Where am I going? Where should I be?

- **Centre Backs**: Where do I aim my passes? Where should I be when we are under pressure?

From these questions we design practices that help our players to learn.

Manu Dorado Real Madrid Academy Coach

Practice 1: Building Up Play and Decision Making in a 5 v 4 Attack

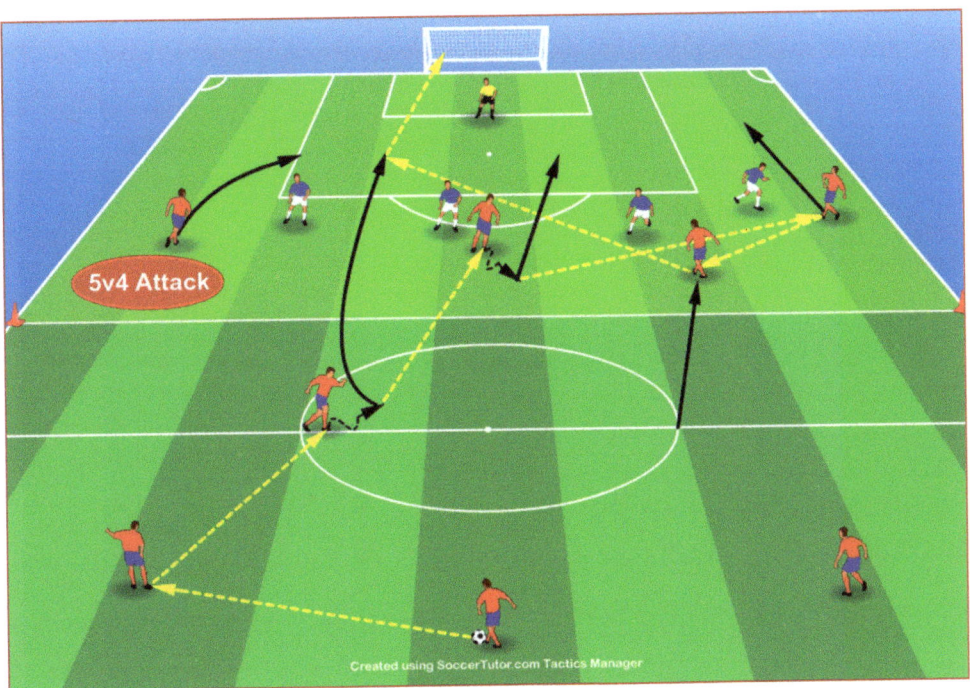

Objective
We work on building up play, decision making and attacking in the final third.

Description
We have 3 defenders, 2 centre midfielders, 2 wingers and 1 forward (3-2-3 formation) playing against 4 defenders (blue) and a goalkeeper.

The ball starts with the defenders and one of them passes to a centre midfielder, who then dribbles forward and passes to one of the 3 attacking players. From that point we have a 5v4 attack in the highlighted area with the players free to make the decisions.

Coaching Point
We want the players to make the right decisions to get in behind the defence and score a goal. The diagram just shows one potential attacking move/combination.

Manu Dorado Real Madrid Academy Coach

In this structured practice we work on specific positions and you can change the formation to suit your team. We have an example below using a 4-4-2. It can easily be adapted to the 4-3-3, 4-2-3-1 or 3-5-2 etc.

You can also adapt the practice to work with players in specific positions, so please consider the following concepts:

Centre Backs

Allow them to join the attack, making runs either through the middle or down the wing (overlapping in cohesion with the midfielders or wingers).

Give them an objective: Play the ball out to the wing quickly.

Full Backs

Add full backs to the practice, using a back 4 instead of a back 3. You could also add 2 blue wingers or centre midfielders.

Give them an objective: Make overlapping runs towards the byline (Example below).

Building Up Play and Decision Making in a 5 v 4 Attack with an Overlapping Full Back

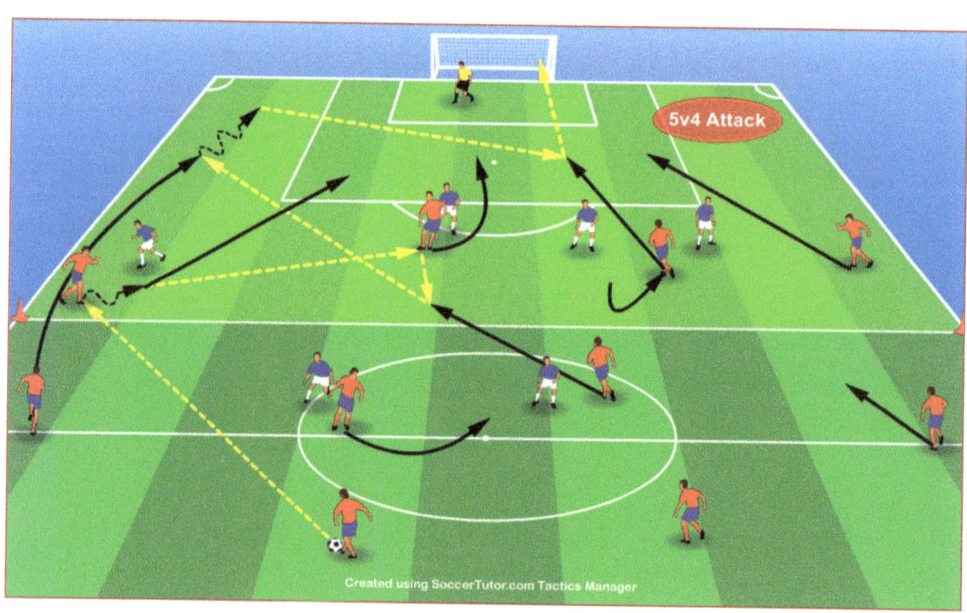

Manu Dorado Real Madrid Academy Coach

Midfielders
Explain what they should be thinking about with and without the ball. This includes covering the lines, moving into the space in front of the centre backs, switching and covering positions with wingers and other midfielders etc.

Wingers
Explain what they should be thinking about with and without the ball. With the ball this includes using the width, isolating defenders 1v1, quick changes of direction and always knowing at least 2 teammate's position on the pitch.

Without the ball includes marking zonal corridors (in front of you), simultaneously with the area inside and moving inside to create space for overlapping runs on the flank.

Centre Forward
Explain what they should be thinking about with and without the ball. With the ball it is important that they play facing the inside of the pitch and always protect the ball.

Without the ball, if the ball is on the flank, they should move towards the penalty spot or the near post for a potential cross and they should look to leave space on the inside.

Manu Dorado Real Madrid Academy Coach

Practice 2: Decision Making on the Flank in a 2 v 2 Small Sided Game

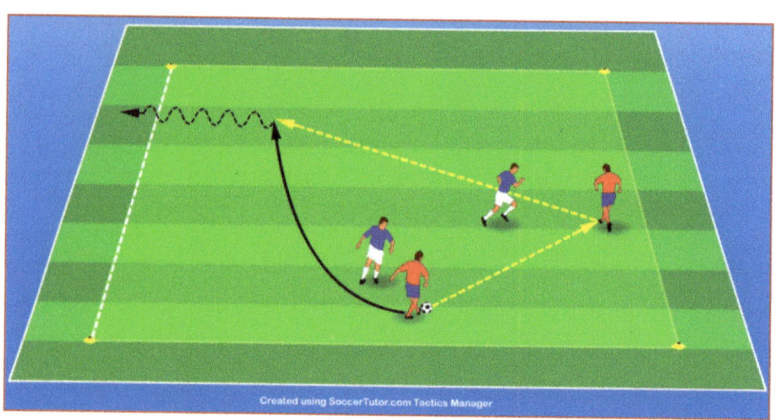

Objective
To develop 1v1/2v2 play with passing, dribbling, attacking the space and defending.

Description
In an area twice as long as it is wide, we work with 2 attacking players and 2 defenders. We play a 2v2 situation and the attackers aim to dribble the ball past the line to score. The only aim for the defenders is to win the ball or kick it out of play.

The players have the freedom to make the decisions for their attack using any passing combinations or feints/moves to beat that they choose.

Coaching Points

We propose possible questions about this with our fellow coaches and all the players:

1. How will we resolve this situation? Watch what the players do and what decisions they make.
2. Which methods have worked? Which have been successful?
3. Have any patterns been repeated?
4. So, how would we solve these situations?

From there, we practice the solutions that we all decided (coaches and players) were "good".

Factors to Consider:

1. The suitability of the practice will depend on the time of year. Can we use this in pre-season or have we detected errors during a competitive game?
2. Depending on the number of players, is it a specific practice for wingers and full backs?
3. Is this the phase of the game you need to work on? In this case it is a practice for the attacking phase which can also be used for the defensive phase.

Practice 3: Correct Distances, Positioning & Movement of the Defensive Line

Objective
To work on the correct distances, positioning and movement of the defensive line.

Description
The 5 attacking players pass the ball between themselves, often switching the play. The 4 defenders must move correctly depending on where the ball is located.

Coaching Points
We propose possible questions about this with our fellow coaches and all the players:

1. What positions should the 4 defenders take when the opponents are advancing with the ball? And if they are advancing down the wing? See what they do in the practice.
2. Which methods have worked? Which have been successful?
3. How do we solve these situations?

And from there, we practice the solutions that we all decided were "good".

Factors to Consider:
1. The suitability of the practice will depend on the time of year. Can we use this in pre-season or have we detected errors during a competitive game?
2. Depending on the number of players, is it a specific practice for defenders?
3. Is this the phase of the game you need to work on? In this case it is a practice for the defensive phase.

Manu Dorado Real Madrid Academy Coach

Practice 4: Attacking Flank Play in a 3 v 3 Small Sided Game

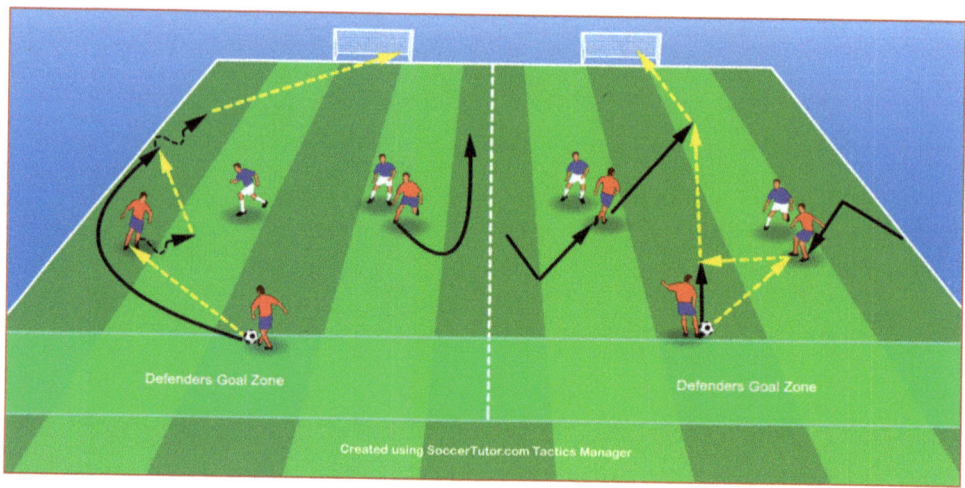

Objective
To develop 1v1/2v1 play, creating space, passing, receiving and player movement.

Description
In this final practice we play free 3v3 small sided games. On each team there are 2 wingers/wide midfielders and 1 central player. The focus is on wide attacking play using moves to beat, numerical advantages and attacking the space.

The diagram shows just 2 examples for how to create and score a goal. The players must consider and try to use all the "working concepts" mentioned in the coaching points.

Coaching Points
In this practice, we work on the following concepts:

1. Try to create a numerical superiority in wide areas.
2. Take the ball to the edge of your zone.
3. Make sure to get in front of your marker and protect the ball.
4. Look to create 2v1 situations whenever possible.
5. Check away from your maker before moving to receive the ball.

CHAPTER 4

FERNANDO GASPAR

China National Team Coach

Former Real Madrid, Benfica, Malaga, Rayo Vallecano, Real Valladolid, Racing Santander & Numancia Coach

FITNESS SPECIALIST COACH PROFILE

Fernando Gaspar
China National Team Fitness Coach

Previous Coaching positions:
- Real Madrid
- SL Benfica
- Malaga CF
- Rayo Vallecano
- Real Valladolid
- Racing Santander
- CD Numancia

Credentials:
- UEFA A Licence
- Bachelor of Physical preparation

Fernando Gaspar China National Team Coach

INTRODUCTION:
PHYSICAL PREPARATION FOR AGES 14-18

The development of the different capabilities of strength, speed, stamina and flexibility must be combined with the cognitive and coordinated training necessary to play football.

The performance of a player in a team sport is dependent on their ability to adapt to situations of uncertainty and interaction.

The player must train by simulating different situations appropriate to their level and the available resources. On this basis, exercises or games are played at a level close to that of competition.

The specific physical requirements of football are divided into 2 behaviours:

1. **High Intensity**: Short duration (strength and speed).
2. **Variable Intensity**: Supporting the connection of different behaviours (stamina).

These elements all depend on the player, playing system and specific position.

14-15 YEAR OLDS

The Age of Inequality:

1. Technical
2. Physical
3. Tactics
4. Transformation

Develop the Player's Autonomy:

There are differences between biological age and chronological age. As a coach, you should do the following:

- Pay Attention to their physical development.
- DO NOT have a general plan, everyone is different.
- Make sure to have COMPETITIVE TRAINING.

"Competition is the best training", so:

- Conduct the training when the players are in a good physical condition, not in a state of exhaustion.
- Develop coordination that is related to and applies to football.
- Develop the players speed specific to football.
- Aerobic resistance and power: different forms of the game and competition.
- Strength through games to develop muscle in general. Avoid excessive muscle gain.
- Flexibility - Avoid injuries.

Why do we need Stamina?

- Delays fatigue.
- Accelerates recovery.
- Maintains the performance of technical and tactical actions.

Why do we need Strength?

- Short 45" actions – very relevant in the game.
- Kicking the ball (shooting and passing).
- 1v1 situations.
- Jumping, changing direction and movement.

Fernando Gaspar China National Team Coach

Why do we need Speed?

- To quickly perform a technical move.
- Moving from one place to another (player movement with and without the ball).
- Speed with which you can perform an action: Reaction time.
- "Tactical aspects are dependent on Speed".

Why do we need Flexibility?

- Muscular flexion-extension in all aspects of the game.
- Dynamic flexibility.
- Relaxation.

16-18 YEAR OLDS

At this age there are fewer inequalities:

How do we work?

Stamina:

Look for real game situations, work on superiority and inferiority in numbers.

- Technical/Tactical Games: Interval training for no more than 45 minutes.
- Distances and Intensities appropriate to a competitive game.
- Intense work split for a maximum of 8 minutes.
- Anaerobic Capacity. Work on situations of superiority and inferiority in numbers for 1-2 minutes max.

Strength:

Introduce strength drills into the tasks to develop strength in a specific area and use competitive exercises.

- Isometric games.
- Standing jumps (competition).
- Work with a medicine ball (2 or 3 kilos for a maximum of 20 minutes).
- Resistance training, always with loads under 50%.

Fernando Gaspar China National Team Coach

Speed:

Use an action specific to football, increasing the difficulty of the work.

- Speed specific to football.
- Short sprints with changes of pace.
- Games against opposition.
- Combined actions that reach completion.

Flexibility:

Avoid injuries and muscular decomposition.

- Mandatory joint mobility work with more stretching before the start of the training session and afterwards.
- Passive Flexibility.
- Active Flexibility.

Can you work on all of the physical preparation with training methods that use a ball?

"In my opinion, if I had ten coaches, one taught me something, three couldn't break me down and six tried to screw with me".
M. Van Basten

"It takes different preparations for the physical, technical and tactical development, all must be trained individually, and this moves us away from the game. The whole is more than the sum of its parts".
A. Giraldez

Fernando Gaspar China National Team Coach

Practices to Improve Conditioning: Stamina, Strength & Speed

Fernando Gaspar China National Team Coach

Dynamic 'Futbol' Conditioning Circuit Training   *25 min*

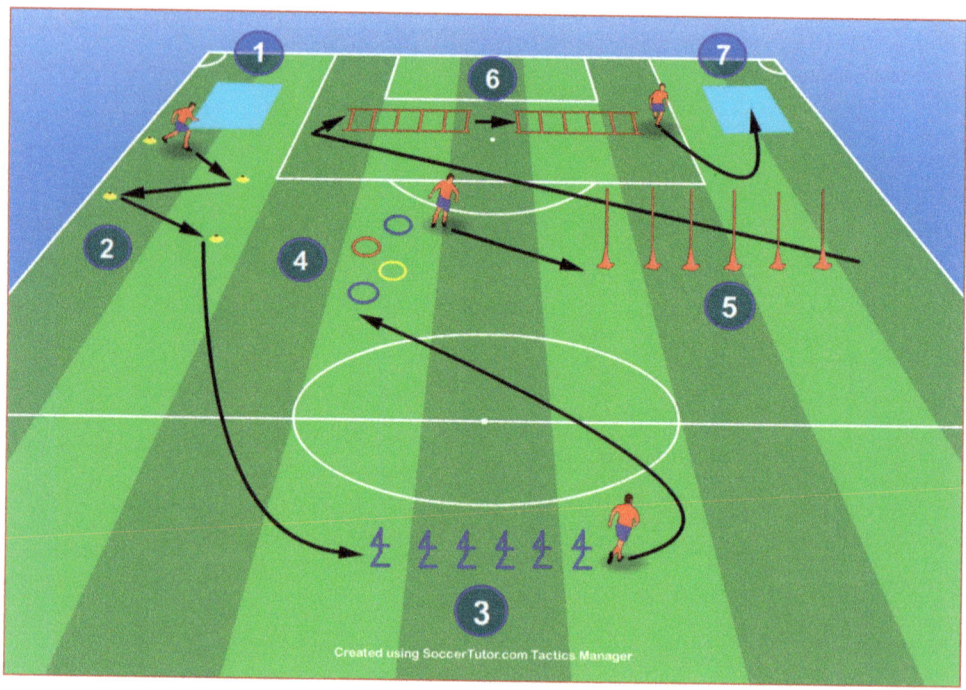

Objective
We work on conditioning including stamina, strength, agility, speed and coordination.

Description
Using half a full sized pitch, all the players work on this conditioning circuit and perform the 7 different elements in sequence. **1** = 10 sit-ups on the mat, **2** = zig-zag run, **3** = jump 6 hurdles, **4** = jump on 1 leg with alternate feet through the rings, **5** = slalom run through the poles, **6** = skip through the 2 ladders and **7** = 10 sit-ups on the mat.

The players perform 7 series (different order of conditioning tasks) like this:
Series 1: 1-2-3-4-5-6-7, **Series 2**: 1-2-3-4-7, **Series 3**: 1-2-4-5-7, **Series 4**: 1-6-4-5-7, **Series 5**: 1-6-5-7 and finish with **2 x reps of Series 6**: 1-2-3-4-5

Coaching Points
1. Make sure the players get sufficient rest time in between each series.
2. Reduce the amount of series the players do depending on the age group.

Fernando Gaspar China National Team Coach

Continuous 1 v 1 Duels and Finishing Practice   *10 min*

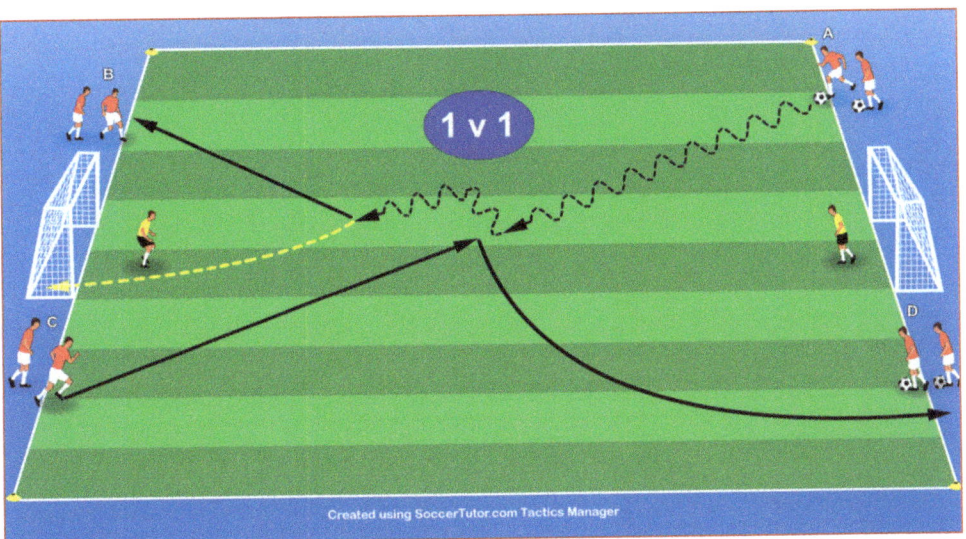

Objective
To develop dribbling, moves to beat and attacking/defending in 1v1 situations while working on conditioning in a continuous practice.

Description
In an area double the size of the penalty area, we work with 8 players. Player A starts by dribbling the ball into the centre. Player C (without a ball) moves to contest Player A in a 1v1 situation.

The attacker aims to score and the defender simply defends the goal. After the 1v1 has finished (a goal is scored or the ball goes out of play), Player A moves to Position B and Player C moves to Position D.

Player D then dribbles the ball forward and starts a 1v1 against Player B. Allow the players 30 seconds rest every 2 minutes.

Coaching Points
1. The player with the ball needs to use a change of pace or direction to beat the defender and score.
2. Do not use more than 8 players because this is a continuous conditioning practice, so we do not want the players standing around waiting.

Fernando Gaspar China National Team Coach

Man to Man Marking 7 v 7 Small Sided Game   15 min

Objective
To develop aerobic resistance within a small sided game with a focus on man to man marking.

Description
In an area up to half a full sized pitch, we play a 7 v 7 small sided game.

The outfield players must each pick an opposition player to man mark. This results in physical competition and aerobic resistance work. The coach can call a change during the game so the players move to man mark another opposition player.

Coaching Points
1. When being man marked, the player with the ball needs to use good body shape and strength to protect the ball (using their arm and body as a barrier to protect the ball).
2. Players should look to receive and then shoot quickly as they will be under tight pressure.

Fernando Gaspar China National Team Coach

Timing Forward Runs and Finishing Practice   10 min

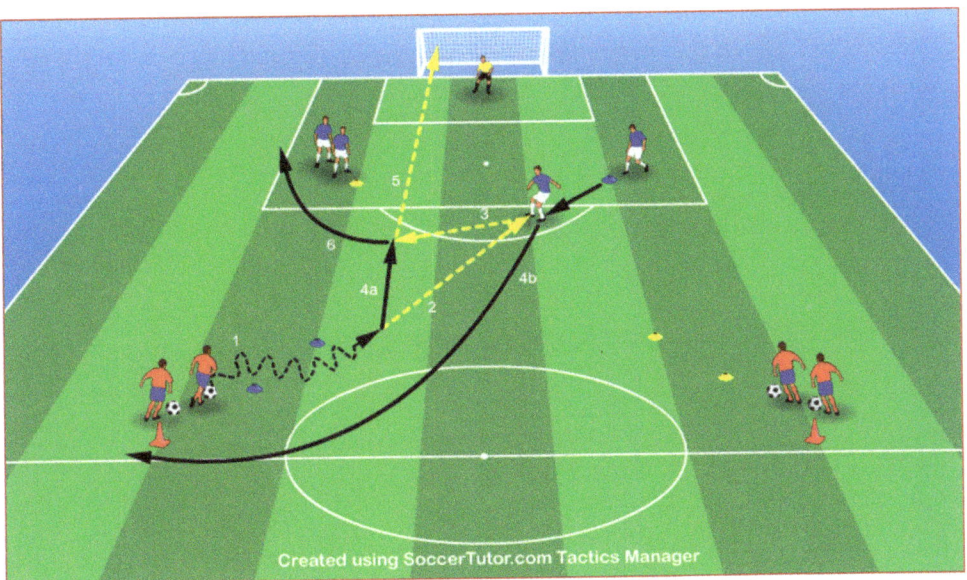

Objective
To develop the timing of forward runs and finishing (in and outside the box) under pressure.

Description
Using half a full sized pitch, there are 4 pairs of players in the positions shown and a goalkeeper.

The first player (red) dribbles through the cones, plays a 1-2 combination with the blue player diagonal to him, moves forward and shoots from outside of the box.

The blue and red players swap positions and the practice continues from the other side.

Coaching Points
1. Players need to use soft touches, keeping the ball close to their feet when dribbling through the cones.
2. The timing of the second pass in the 1-2 combination is very important, so that the player moving forward does not have to slow down to receive the ball and shoot.
3. Progress to shoot with 1 touch to force the need for a quality weight of pass.

Fernando Gaspar China National Team Coach

Global 'Futbol' Specific Circuit Training   15 min

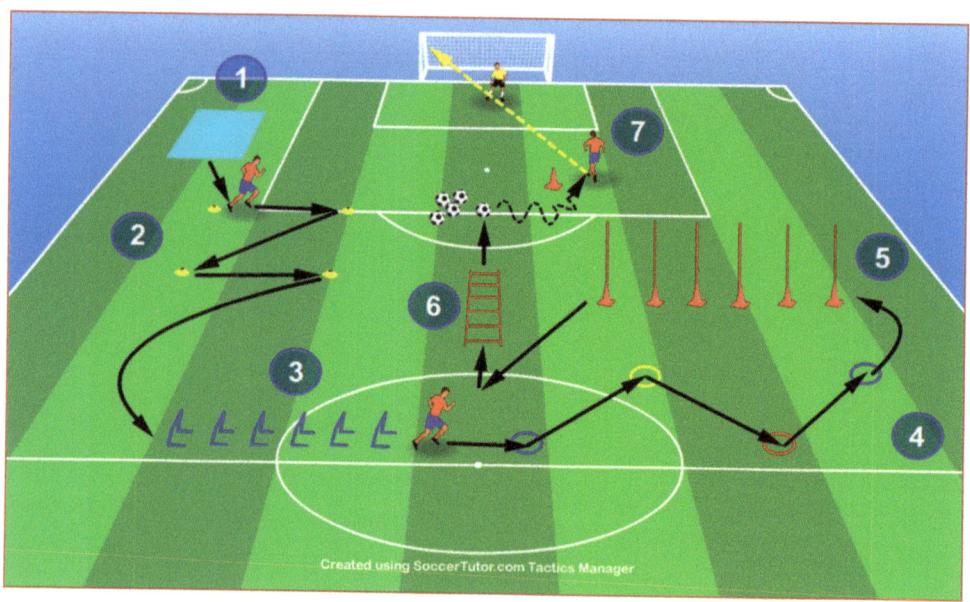

Objective
We work on conditioning with a focus on the strength and stamina components.

Description
Using half a full sized pitch, the players work on this conditioning circuit and perform the 7 different elements in sequence.

1 = 10 sit-ups on the mat, **2** = sharp changes of direction **3** = jump 6 hurdles, **4** = 3 high jumps in each ring (12 total), **5** = zig-zag run through the poles, **6** = skip through the speed ladder and **7** = Collect a ball, dribble round the cone and shoot at goal.

The players perform 5 series in the same number sequence (1-2-3-4-5-6-7).

Coaching Points
1. Make sure the players get sufficient rest time in between each series.
2. Reduce the amount of series the players do depending on the age group.

Fernando Gaspar China National Team Coach

Circuit Training with Combination Play & Finishing   15 min

Objective
We work on passing, combination play, player movement and timing of runs within a conditioning circuit.

Description
Using half a full sized pitch, the players are divided into 4 different areas. In area 1, the players do 5 sit-ups, in area 2 they skip through the speed ladder, in area 3 they jump 5 hurdles and in area 4 the players hop using alternate feet through the speed rings. Each player must perform their designated exercise before taking part in the passing combination.

The first player in area 1 starts the circuit by passing the ball to the area 2 player, who passes to the area 3 player. Player 1 makes a curved run around the cone into the box (black line) and Player 2 makes an overlapping run on the flank to receive the next pass back from Player 3.

Player 3 (blue line) and Player 4 (orange line) both make curved runs into the box as well and Player 2 completes the circuit by crossing the ball into the box for one of the 3 players in there who try to score a goal.

Coaching Point
The coach has to coordinate the movement of the 4 players to make sure the timing of the passes and the movement is right.

Strength, Power and Finishing Practice

10 min

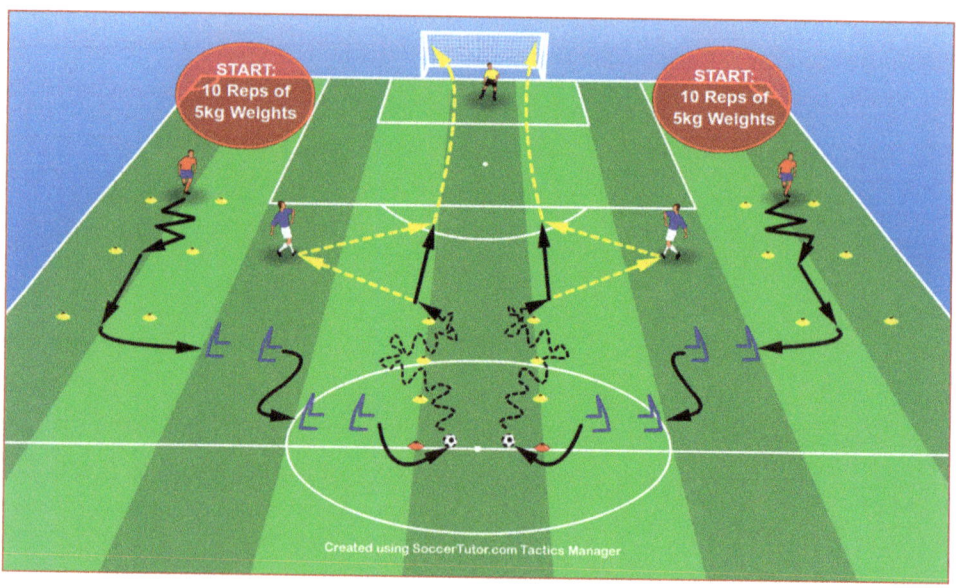

Objective
To develop strength, power, explosive power and finishing.

Description
We split the players into 2 groups with 2 serving players (blue) positioned as shown. We place the cones and hurdles as shown and work on a strength and power circuit with finishing.

This practice works as a competition in pairs and each pair should complete 4 repetitions.

Firstly, both players must perform 10 reps of 5kg weights. They then start the circuit by zig-zag running to halfway through the cones and then sprint straight to the end.

The players then run to the hurdles where they must perform 2 standing jumps, then move to the next 2 hurdles and perform 2 standing jumps again.

To complete the circuit, the players collect a ball, dribble through the cones, play a 1-2 combination with the blue player and shoot at goal (first one to score gets a point).

Coaching Point
Make sure to use standing jumps for the hurdles with feet together.

Fernando Gaspar China National Team Coach

Practices to Improve Speed, Agility Coordination & Strength

Fernando Gaspar China National Team Coach

Coordinated Runs and Movement with Crossing & Finishing

20 min

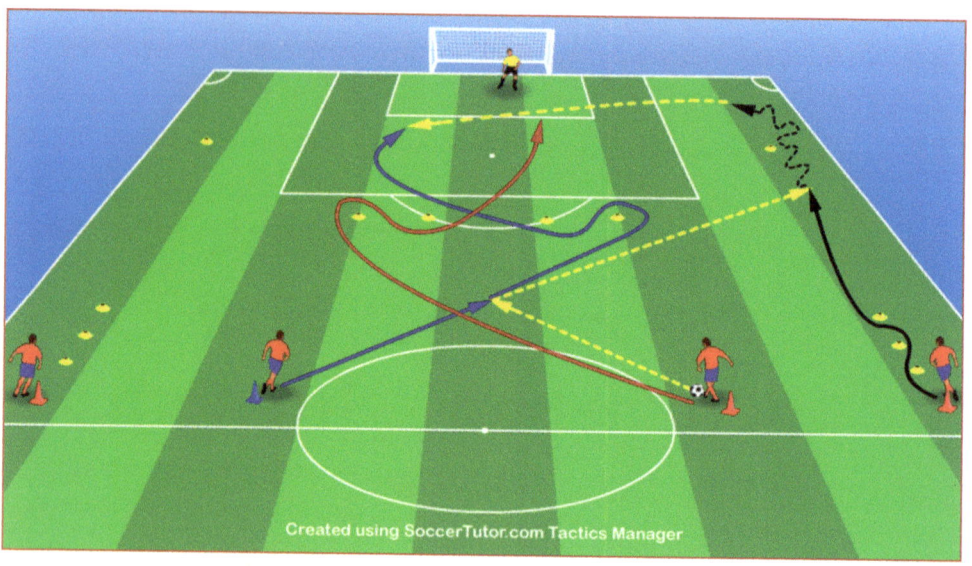

Objective
To develop acceleration, speed, coordination, coordinated movements, crossing and finishing.

Description
We have 4 starting positions and the combination is between 3 players. One middle player starts by passing the ball diagonally into the middle for a teammate who has made a diagonal run forward.

The second player passes the ball out wide and both players make the movements shown (run in between the yellow cones - one runs to the near post and the other to the far post).

The wide player runs in between the cones, runs forward, receives the pass, dribbles forwar towards the byline and crosses for the 2 players in the middle.

Coaching Points
1. The key to this practice is the coordinated timing of runs to the passes and the final cross.
2. When making the diagonal runs in the centre, players need to be aware to avoid collisions.
3. The second pass should be with 1 touch to speed up play.

Fernando Gaspar China National Team Coach

One-Two Combination, Dribbling and Finishing in a Coordination & Speed Exercise

8 min

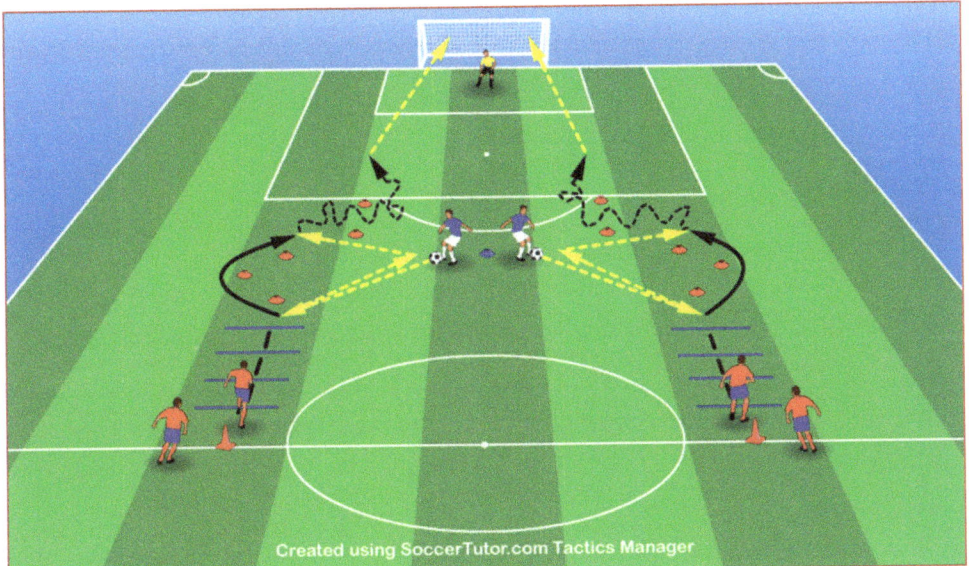

Objective
To develop coordination, speed, one-two combination play, dribbling and finishing.

Description
We use half a full sized pitch and have lines of players on both sides, 2 blue support players and a goalkeeper. The players on both sides set off at the same time.

The players perform skips over the 4 poles on the ground. They then play a 1-2 combination with the blue support players and run round the 3 cones to receive the pass back.

After receiving the pass, both players dribble the ball through the cone gates, dribble forward and shoot at goal.

Coaching Points
1. The support player's second pass needs to be well timed and weighted in front of the player to run onto without breaking stride.
2. For the dribbling section, players should use soft touches to maximise control of the ball.
3. This whole exercise should be done at high speed, as if in a real game situation.

Fernando Gaspar China National Team Coach

Attacking Combination Play on the Flank in a Speed and Acceleration Practice

20 min

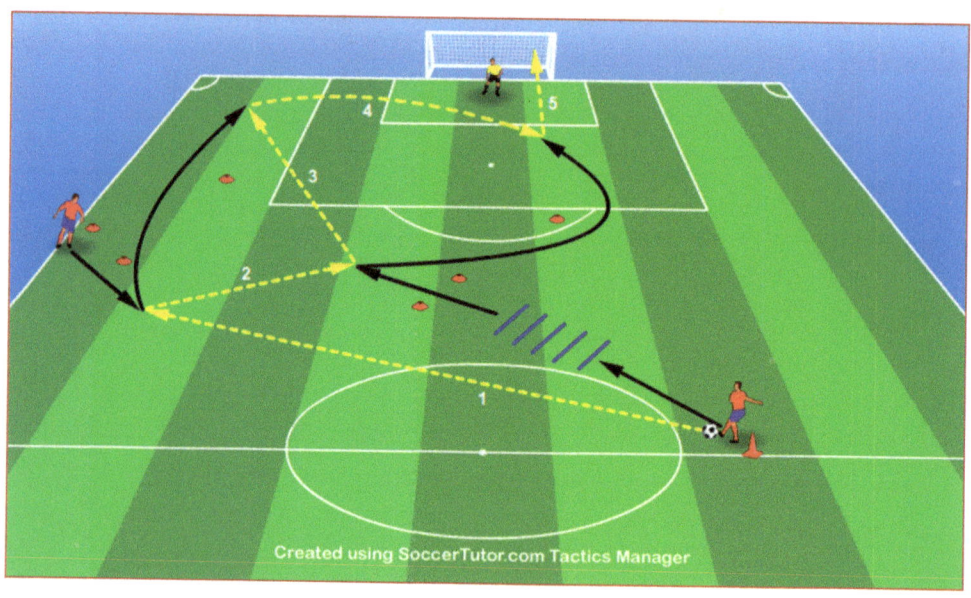

Objective
To develop speed, coordination and timing for different movements (short and long) in an attacking combination.

Description
We use half a full sized pitch and mark out the cones in the positions shown. Perform the practice on both sides of the pitch.

The player with the ball passes it out wide and skips between the poles, emerges at speed and receives the ball back from his teammate who has moved inside to play the 1-2 combination.

The first player then passes the ball into the space on the flank for the second player to run onto. After he has passed the ball, he runs around the last cone and moves into the penalty area. The player with the ball crosses the ball for the first player to finish.

Coaching Points
1. The players need to use short and explosive acceleration in this practice.
2. The timing of the passes or cross to the run is important for the flow of the exercise.

Fernando Gaspar China National Team Coach

Speed and Agility in a 1 v 1 Duel with Finishing   10 min

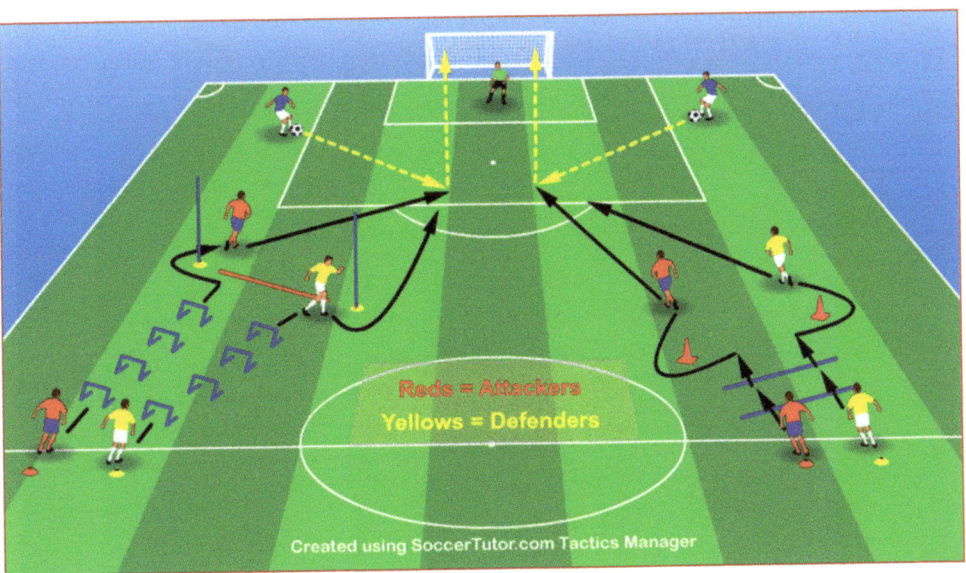

Objective
To develop acceleration, agility and finishing in a 1v1 situation.

Description
On both sides we have a 1v1 situation (red vs yellow). Both players must run at maximum speed around one of the two circuits.

The yellow player must react quickly, approaching the attacker to prevent the goal. The red player must get out in front to receive the ball in the box and shoot.

There are 4 series in each circuit with recovery time between each series.

Circuit 1 (left): Jump over 4 hurdles, run around the pole and sprint into the box.
Circuit 2 (right): Skip over 2 poles on the floor, run around the cone and sprint into the box.

Coaching Point
When turning/changing direction, the players should bend their knees and drop one shoulder and then push off on one foot to accelerate.

Fernando Gaspar China National Team Coach

Quick Reactions & Finishing in a 3 v 3 Practice   7 min

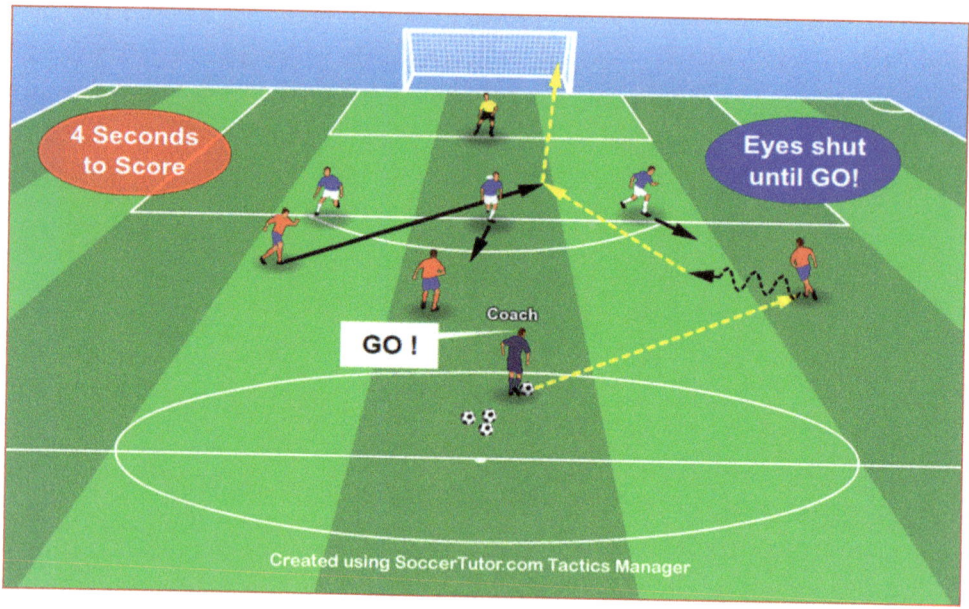

Objective
To develop speed of play and quick decision making (attacking & defending in a 3v3 situation).

Description
We use half a full sized pitch and work with 3 attackers (red), 3 defenders (blue) and a goalkeeper. We play 3v3 with the 3 defenders starting in the penalty area with their eyes closed and 3 attackers face them.

The practice starts when the coach calls "GO" and plays a pass to one of the 3 attackers. The 3 defenders open their eyes and must react quickly. The attackers have 4 seconds to score and if they are unable to do this, the practice starts again with the coach.

Change the team roles halfway through the practice (after 3.5 minutes).

Coaching Points
1. In this practice we give the attacking players complete freedom of decision making to use any method they choose to try and score the goal within the time limit.
2. It is important to give the players time to recuperate between each attack.

Fernando Gaspar China National Team Coach

Possession Play & 3 v 2 Fast Break Attacks

15 min

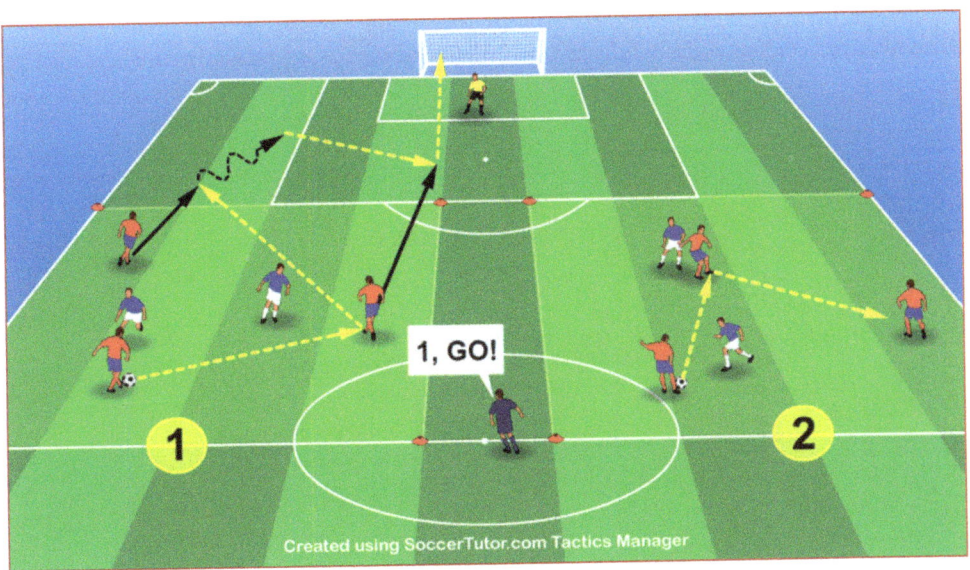

Objective
To develop speed of play and quick decision making in specific situations (3v2).

Description
We use half a full sized pitch and mark out 2 zones as shown. In each zone there is a 3v2 situation and at first the 3 players (red) just maintain possession against the 2 defenders.

On the coaches signal, the team in possession launch a quick attack and try to score past the goalkeeper, using their numerical advantage.

Perform 10 repetitions with recovery time in between. Change team roles halfway through.

Progression
Increase the player's motivation by dividing the players into 2 teams competing against each other. The team that has scored the most goals at the end of the practice are the winners.

Coaching Points
1. Give the players freedom of decision making for the attacks.
2. Only stop to evaluate the players performance if they score a goal.

Fernando Gaspar China National Team Coach

Acceleration and Finishing in 1 v 1 Duels

15 min

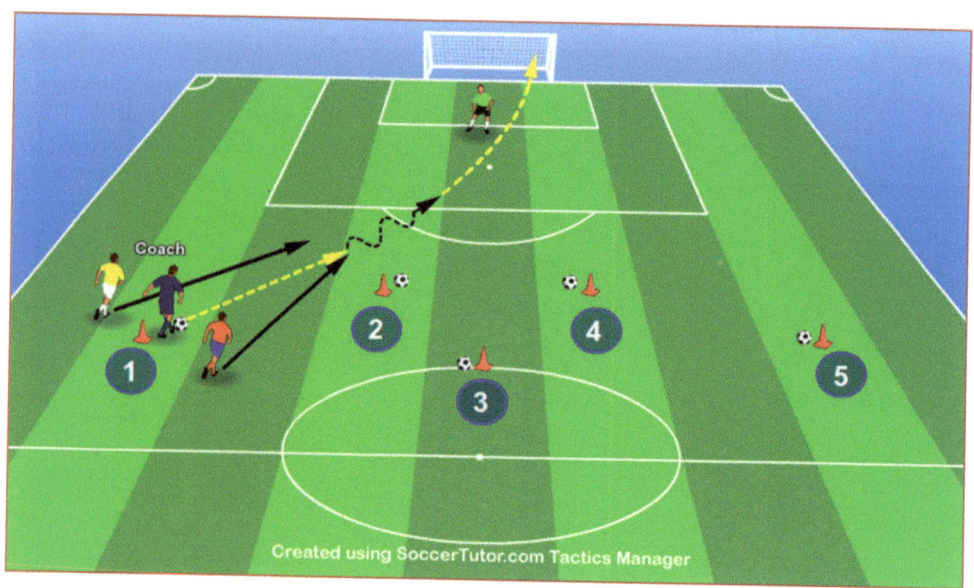

Objective
To work on acceleration, protecting the ball and finishing in a specific game situation (1v1).

Description
Using half a full sized pitch, we mark out the 5 positions shown in the diagram. 2 players perform the exercise in all 5 positions, starting with the first.

The coach stands in between the 2 players and throws/passes the ball fin front of them. The objective for both players is to gain possession of the ball, protect it and score a goal.

The player that does not get to the ball first becomes the defender and tries to stop his opponent from scoring.

Perform 10 repetitions; 2 from each position with recovery time in between each repetition.

Coaching Points
1. Monitor the correct technique for explosive acceleration.
2. Players need to use their body as a barrier between the ball and the defender (shielding).

Fernando Gaspar China National Team Coach

Acceleration and Attacking Flank Play 2 v 2 Duel — 15 min

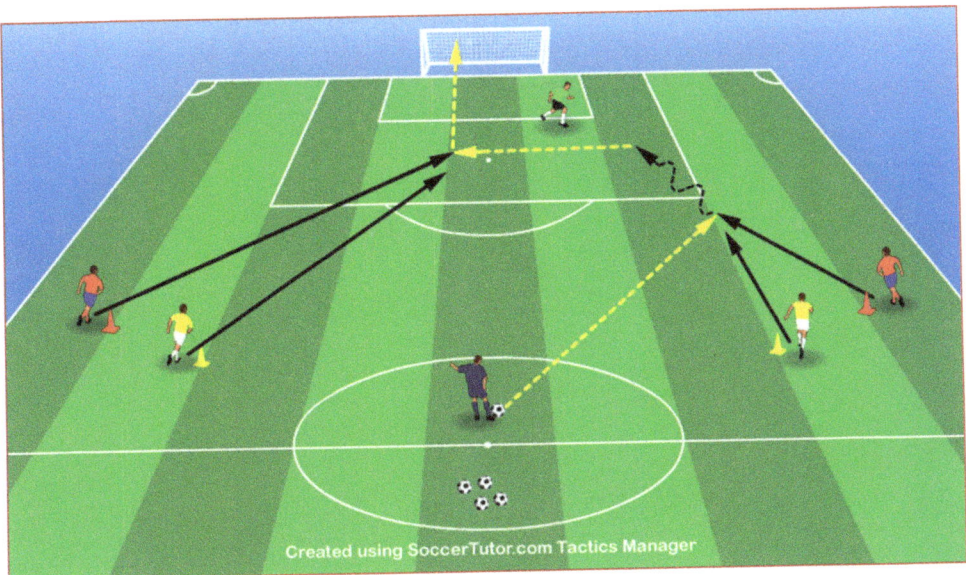

Objective
Speed of acceleration, gestural and mental speed in specific situations.

Description
In the same area, we now have 2 pairs of players working with the coach. The red players are the attackers and the yellow players are the defenders.

The coach passes the ball out wide to either side and the 2 players (1v1) on that side race to get to the ball. The attacking player can use his teammate in the attack (as shown in the diagram) in order to score a goal in the shortest time possible and the other defender must track to defend.

Perform 8 repetitions of this 2v2 situation with recovery time in between each repetition.

Coaching Points
1. Allow the players freedom to decide what action to take in order to reach the objective.
2. The attackers should aim to finish the attack quickly and pick the right option to do this.
3. Also focus on the quick reactions and cohesion of the defenders as they try to stop the attack.

Fernando Gaspar China National Team Coach

Technical: Receiving and Finishing Under Pressure in the Penalty Area

6 min

Objective
To develop receiving and finishing quickly in the penalty area and defending in a 1v1.

Description
Within the penalty area, we have 1 player on the edge (red) and 2 players either side of the goal ready to feed passes in. There are 2 defenders (yellow) in the positions shown.

The ball is passed as the attacker moves forward and he has to score within 3 seconds of receiving. The defenders start 4 yards away and one of them moves across to stop the attacker from scoring. This creates a 1v1 situation for a quick finishing exercise.

Each attacker should perform 6 repetitions and the defenders take turns.

Coaching Points
1. The first touch needs to be out in front and in the opposite direction to the defender.
2. The defender should aim to move across quickly and make physical contact with the attacker to either stop the shot or at least effect it.

Fernando Gaspar China National Team Coach

Attacking at Speed and Finishing from Different Angles in 1 v 1 Duels

8 min

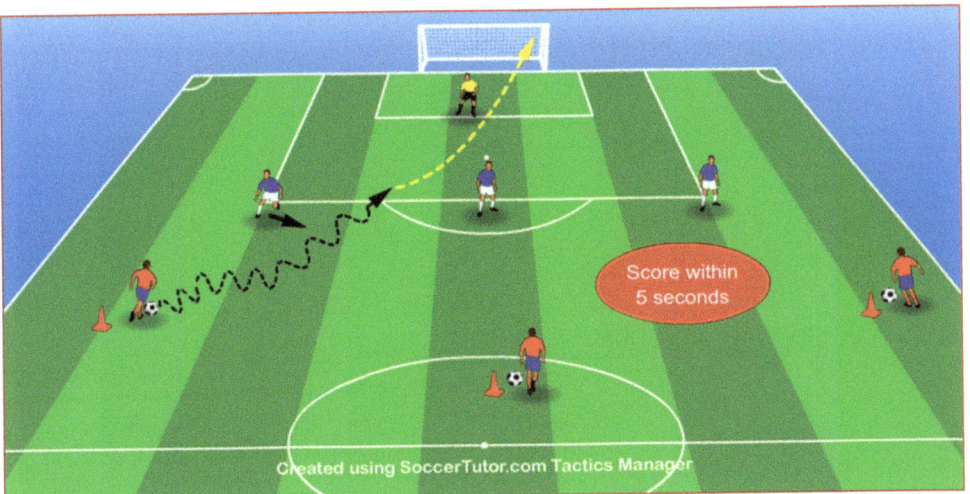

Objective
To develop attacking/defending in 1v1 situations with the focus on finishing the attack quickly.

Description
We mark out 3 positions in half a full sized pitch and practice 1v1 situations. The attackers (red) face the defender opposite them (blue). The players can simply take turns to start their 1v1 or the coach can give the players numbers and call them out randomly.

The attacker starts by dribbling at speed and must score within 5 seconds. The defender tries to stop the attacker scoring (see coaching points). Each attacker performs 6 repetitions.

Progressions
1. We can perform this practice from specific positions to improve the performance of those players or change the zones to give the players more variety.

2. Make it a competition with 2 teams competing to score the most goals.

Coaching Points
1. The attackers need to keep the ball close to their feet using feints and quick changes of direction to get past the defender and score.

2. Defenders need to adopt the 'surfboard' position and adapt to the speed of the attacker.

3. The defender should have the front of their body angled away from the goal.

Fernando Gaspar China National Team Coach

Coordination and Speed of Footwork Exercise   *12 min*

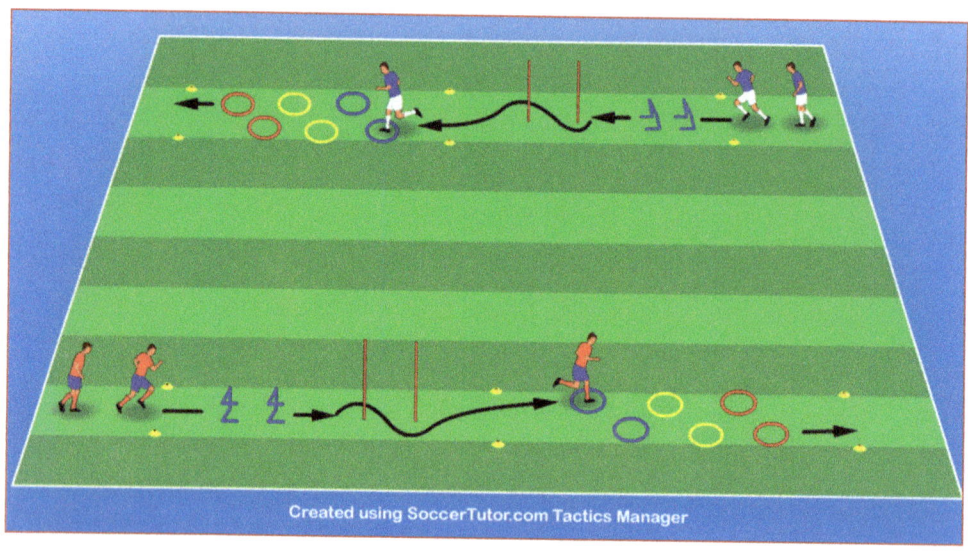

Objective
To develop coordination and speed of footwork and changing direction.

Description
In this exercise we have a competition between 2 teams with the fastest team the winner. The circuit is 30 yards long and each player in the teams completes 4 repetitions. Use a minimum of 45 seconds recovery time between each series.

The players start by jumping over the 2 hurdles, run in between the poles with 2 changes of direction, run through the 2 cones, hop through the speed rings from left to right leg alternately and run through the final 2 cones.

Progression
Add a ball and a mini goal at the end of the circuit for the players to take a shot.

Coaching Points
1. Make sure the hurdles used are the appropriate size for the age of the players.
2. When changing direction through the poles, the players should slow down, bend their knees and then push off one foot to accelerate in the opposite direction.
3. Balance is very important when transferring from one leg to the other through the rings.

Fernando Gaspar China National Team Coach

Quick Reactions and Finishing Speed Circuit   *15 min*

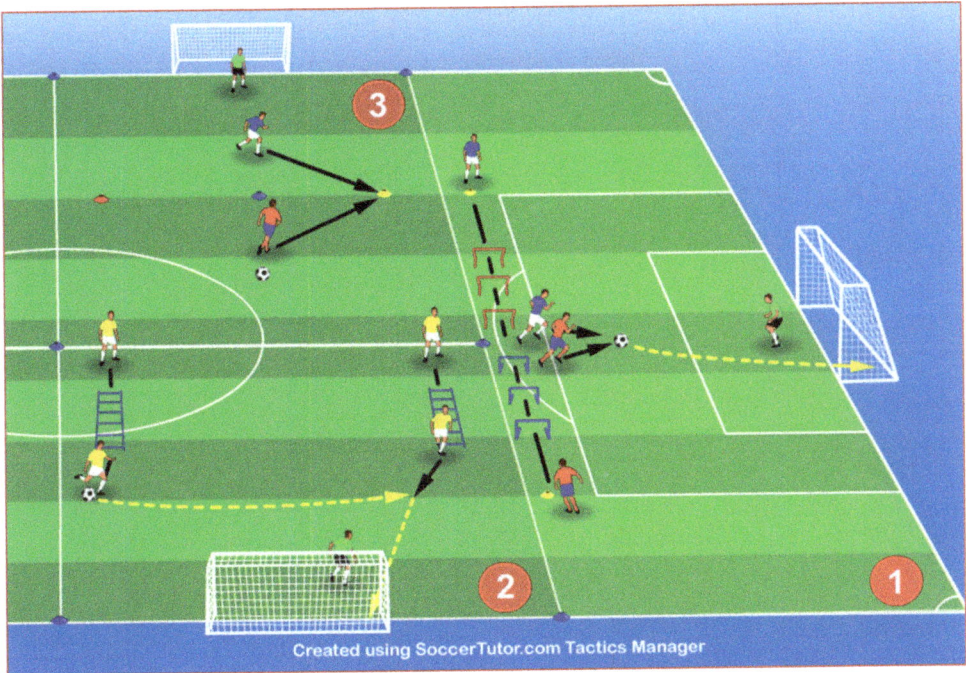

Objective
This circuit is used to train coordination, foot speed and quick reactions with agility.

Description
As shown in the diagram, there are 3 zones marked out using half a full sized pitch where we have football specific speed exercises.

Zone 1 - Both players start at the same time (red & blue) and jump over their 3 hurdles. The players then race to the ball (1v1) and try to score past the goalkeeper.

Zone 2 - On the left, we play a game of "mirrors" between an attacker and a defender in a 1v1 situation. The attacker sprints to one of the 3 cones and the defender must mirror the movement (as shown in the diagram). After 3 repetitions they play a normal 1v1 with the attacker trying to score in the goal with the goalkeeper.

Zone 3 - The 2 players start at the same time and they both run through the ladder before one plays a cross to the other who finishes (as shown in the diagram).

Fernando Gaspar China National Team Coach

Speed, Agility, Awareness and Decision Making Pattern of Play

8 min

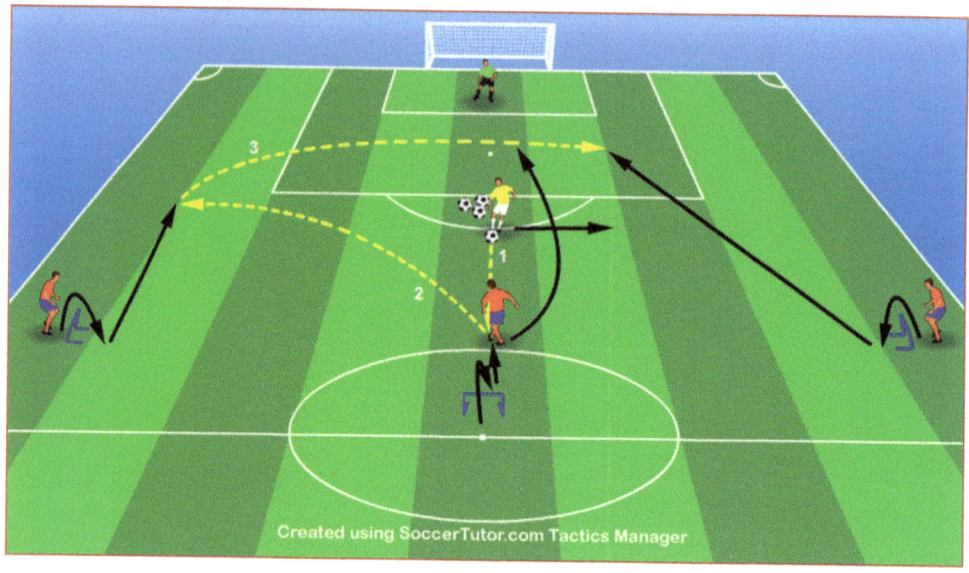

Objective
We work on speed, agility, vision, awareness and decision making in a specific pattern of play.

Description
Using half a full sized pitch, we mark out 3 positions where each player has a hurdle in front of them. At first, the players jump over the hurdle 3 times and then repeat this sequence again (with recovery time in between).

The yellow player then passes ball to the player in the centre who moves forward to receive. The yellow player then moves to one side (as shown in the diagram) and the player in the centre must play the ball to the OPPOSITE wing than that indicated.

The player on the opposite wing and the player in the centre should run forwards to attack the cross into the penalty area, but they should not sprint more than 15 yards.

Repeat the series 4 times and rotate the player roles each time (include recovery time).

Progression
Add 1 or 2 defenders to make it more similar to a real game situation.

Fernando Gaspar China National Team Coach

Technical: Ball Control and Passing in a Continuous Circuit

10 min

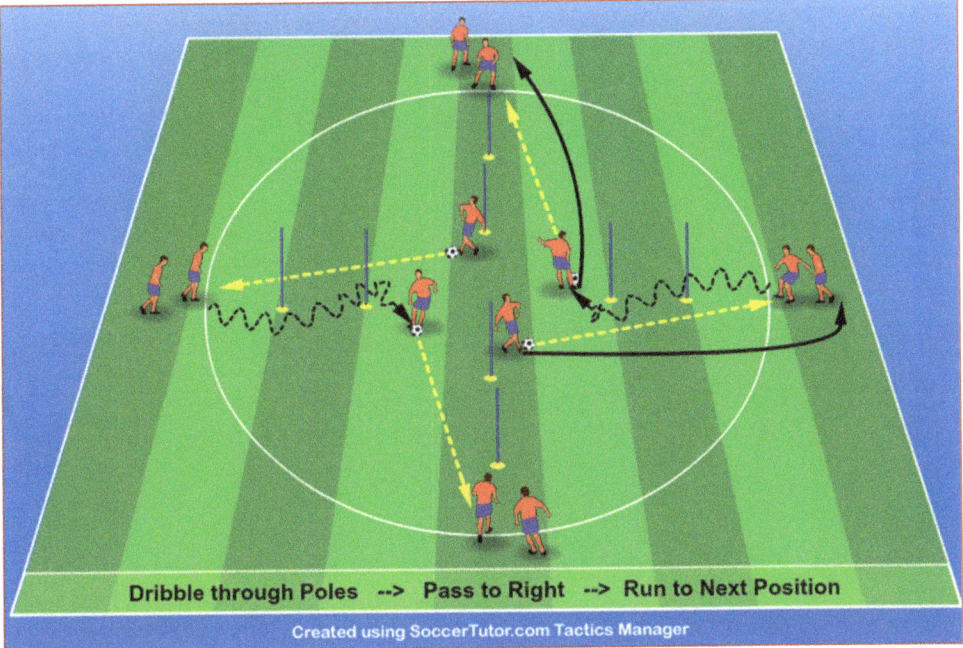

Objective
This conditioning drill also works on ball control, passing and player movement.

Description
We have 4 lines of players with each group 5-10 yards apart with the poles in the positions shown. We perform various different exercises with varying time limits:

4 min - Sprint straight to the middle and move to the line on the right.
2 min - Slalom through the poles and change of direction/pace joining the line on the left.
4 min - We give a ball to each line (4 in total) and dribble through the poles, pass to right, then run to next position (this is represented in the diagram).

Coaching Points
1. Players need to all work at the same speed to maintain the rhythm of the practice.
2. When changing direction through the poles, the players should slow down, bend their knees and then push off one foot to accelerate in the opposite direction.

Fernando Gaspar China National Team Coach

Speed and Agility Practice with Accurate Passing   12 min

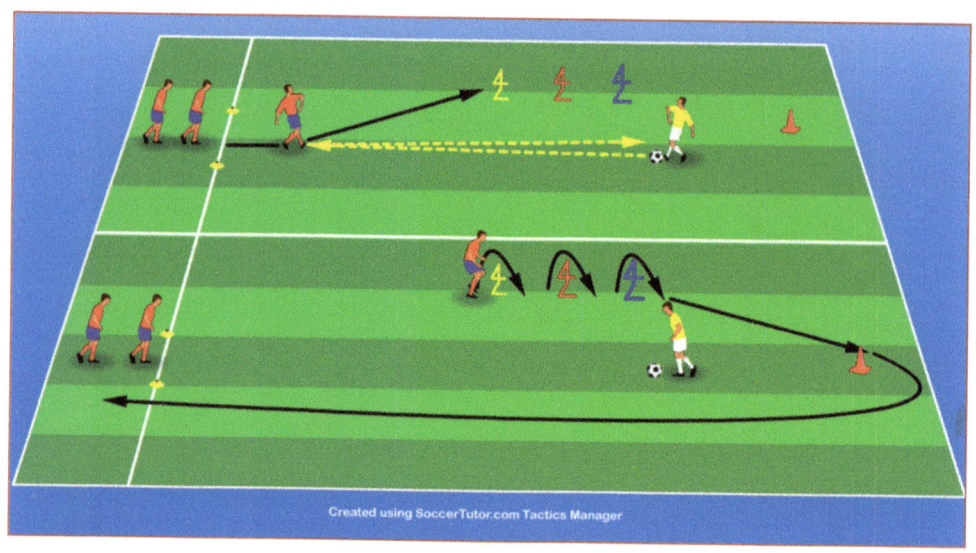

Objective
This practice works on speed, agility and passing. It can also be used as a warm up.

Description
The players line up in groups and the goalkeepers (or support players) stand 5-8 yards in front of them. The sequence remains the same, but we change the type of pass. There is 1 minute recovery time in between each 3 minute series.

3 min - The goalkeeper (or support player) passes to the player along the ground who passes back with 1 touch. The player then runs to and jumps over the 3 different sized hurdles (low, medium and high), before finally sprinting to the cone and then returning to the start position.

3 min - The same exercise, but the goalkeeper (or support player) throws the ball up to his teammate who returns the ball with a volley back into the hands.

3 min - The same exercise, but the goalkeeper (or support player) throws the ball for the player to head back to him.

Variation
Instead of only using hurdles we can use speed rings instead or in addition.

Fernando Gaspar China National Team Coach

Playing Under Physical Pressure in a 4 v 4 (+5) Possession Game

10 min

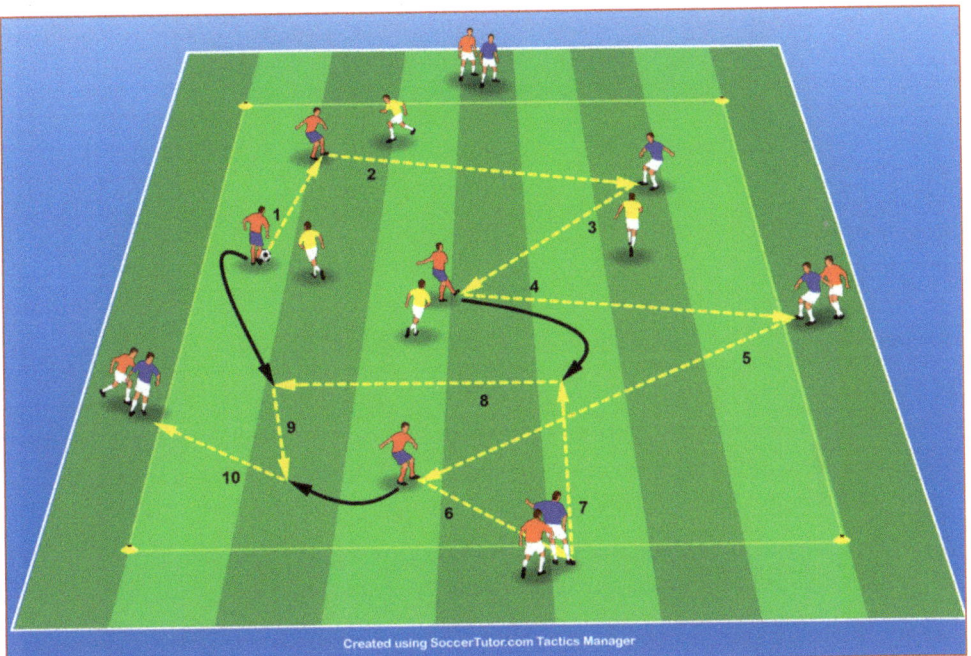

Objective
To develop passing, possession, creating space and support play under pressure.

Description
In an area 20 x 20 yards we have a 4v4 situation inside. There are an additional 5 support players (blue) who play with the team in possession. 4 of the support players who are outside the area are put under pressure by the orange players who provide light resistance by tugging the players' shirts.

If the defending team (yellow in diagram) win the ball and manage to complete 5 passes, stop the practice and change the team roles.

If the defending team do not manage to win the ball and are unable to prevent 10 passes, stop the practice and start again with the same team roles. The players are not allowed to pass more than 3 times to a utility player within a sequence of 10 passes.

Coaching Points
1. Monitor the amount of physical pressure applied to the outside players.
2. Moving to receive, players should be half-turned, aware of teammates and opposition.
3. Constant movement is needed to fully exploit the numerical advantage.

Fernando Gaspar China National Team Coach

Coordination, Agility and Finishing Speed Race   **10 min**

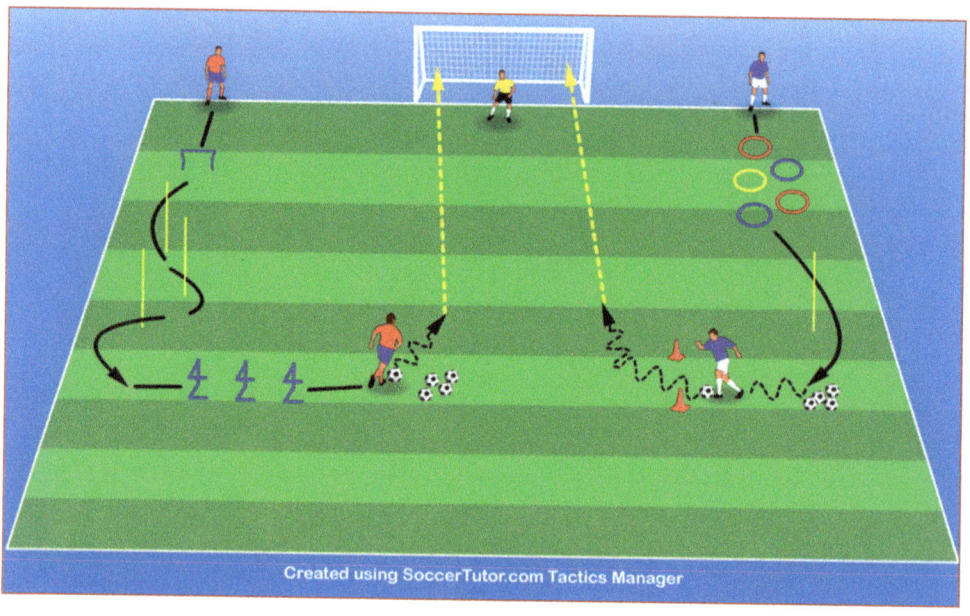

Objective
We work on finishing following strength, agility and coordination components.

Description
We divide the group into 2, make it a competition and count the number of goals. On one side the players jump over 1 hurdle, slalom through the poles, then jump 3 more hurdles before collecting a ball and shooting at goal.

On the other side the players hop from one foot to the other through the speed rings, run around the pole on the outside and collect a ball. They then dribble through the cones and shoot at goal.

The teams should swap sides halfway through so they each get 5 minutes working on each side. The players can recuperate while they are waiting to set off.

Coaching Points
1. The correct body shape to balance through the speed rings should be monitored.
2. Players should aim for good height over the hurdles with their feet together.

Fernando Gaspar China National Team Coach

Technical: Escaping the Marker in a Continuous Finishing Practice

15 min

Objective
To develop the movement to check away from a marker, timed to receive and finish quickly.

Description
In an area roughly double the size of the penalty area, there are 8 utility players (numbered) who stand in positions around the outside with 1 or 2 balls each.

Inside the zone we have a 1v1 situation (1 defender and 1 attacker). The coach calls out a number and that utility player must then try to pass to the attacker. The sole aim for the attacker is to escape their marker by checking away and then accelerate in the opposite direction to receive the pass and finish first time.

The attacker works for 30 seconds before swapping roles with the defender. They then both swap with 2 utility players. The players can recuperate while they are a utility player.

Coaching Point
The focus here is for the attacker to check away from the marker before moving to receive.

Fernando Gaspar China National Team Coach

Jumping Power, Ball Control and Finishing Practice

8 min

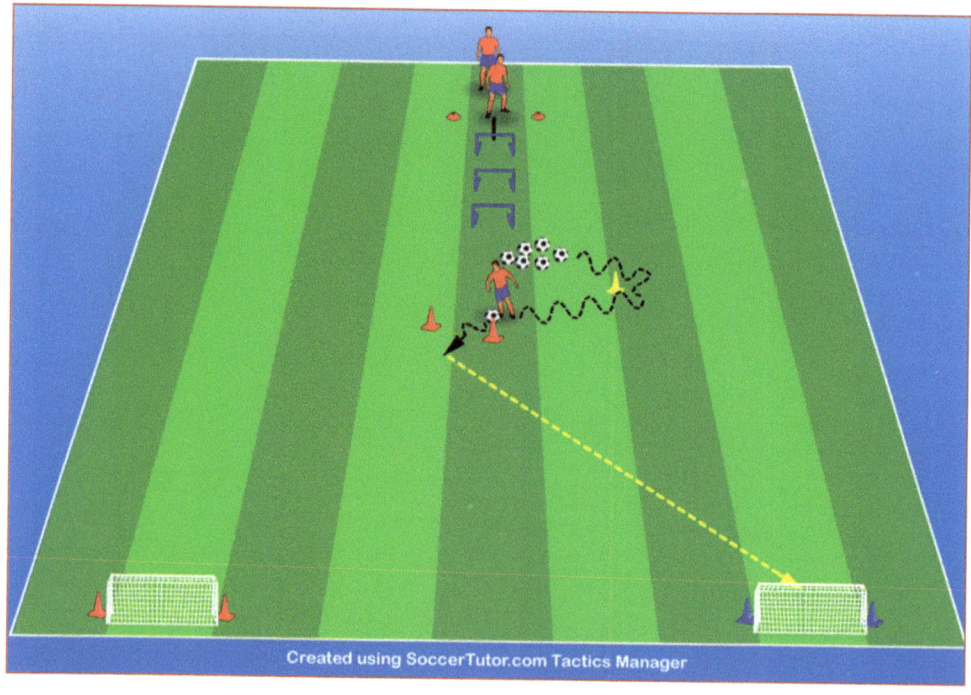

Objective
We work on jumping (agility & power), ball control and finishing.

Description
We work with 1 line of players. They start by jumping over 3 hurdles with their feet together looking for maximum height. They collect a ball, dribble around the outside of the yellow cone, through the 2 red cones before shooting into one of the two mini goals.

If the player misses the goal, they must sprint at full speed to one of the cones at the side of that same mini goal. Work for 8 minutes with a break every 2 minutes for 30 seconds.

Coaching Points
1. The coach can call out the colour of the goal to shoot in to improve vision/awareness.
2. Players should aim for good height over the hurdles with their feet together.

Fernando Gaspar China National Team Coach

Explosive Power, Coordination and Heading Practice

10 min

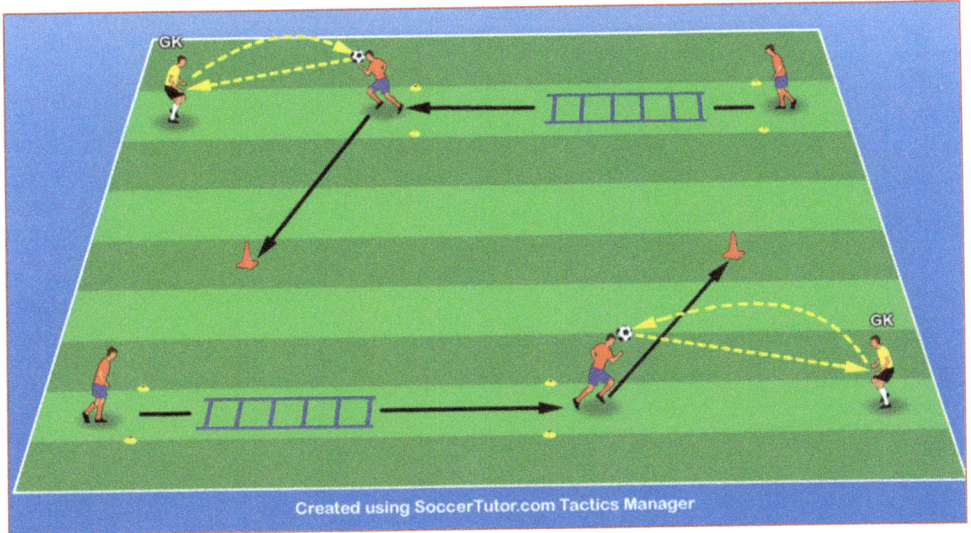

Objective
To develop coordination, explosive power and accurate heading.

Description
We have 2 lines and the yellow cones are 10 yards apart. The players perform different coordination exercises with the 4 metre speed ladder. Keep changing this, with examples such as 2 inside touches – 1 outside, 2 inside touches - 2 outside touches etc.

When the player reaches the end of the ladder, he sprints forwards and the goalkeeper throws the ball to him. He heads it back before changing direction and accelerating towards the cone.

Work for 2 minutes followed by a 30 second rest/break. Repeat 4 times.

Coaching Points
1. With the varying techniques on the speed ladder, players need good rhythm and quick feet to accomplish the tasks - this can be monitored and improved.
2. Both sprinting parts should be done at full speed.

Fernando Gaspar China National Team Coach

Speed and Coordination Exercise

10 min

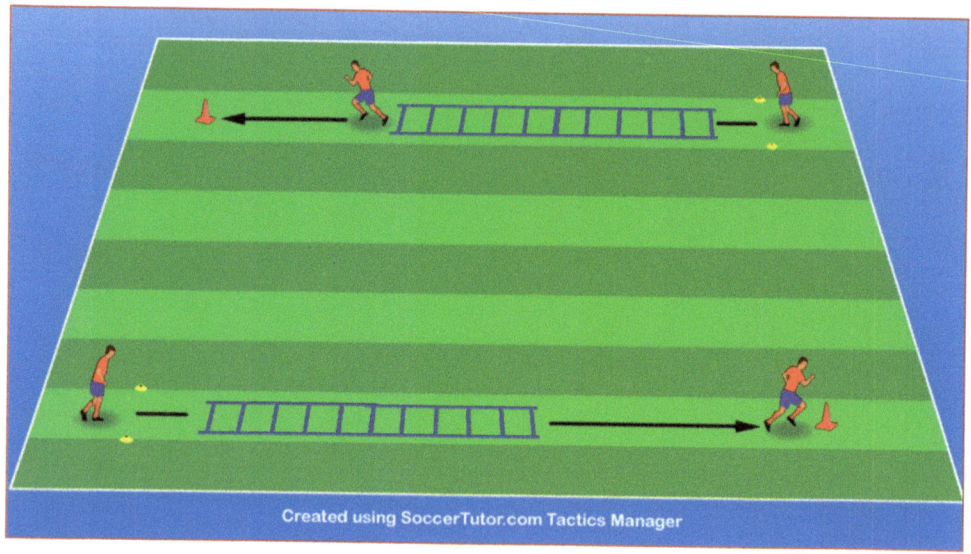

Objective
To develop coordination, acceleration and explosive power.

Description
This is very similar to the previous drill, but this time there are 2 x 4 metre ladders joined together and the players simply sprint forwards to the cone after finishing the ladder work.

Work for 2 minutes followed by a 30 second rest/break. Repeat 4 times.

Coaching Point
As well as the technical requirements and need for quick feet, endurance is now required as the ladder part is twice the length.

Fernando Gaspar China National Team Coach

Possession and Speed of Play in a 3 v 3 Small Sided Game with Cone Gates

10 min

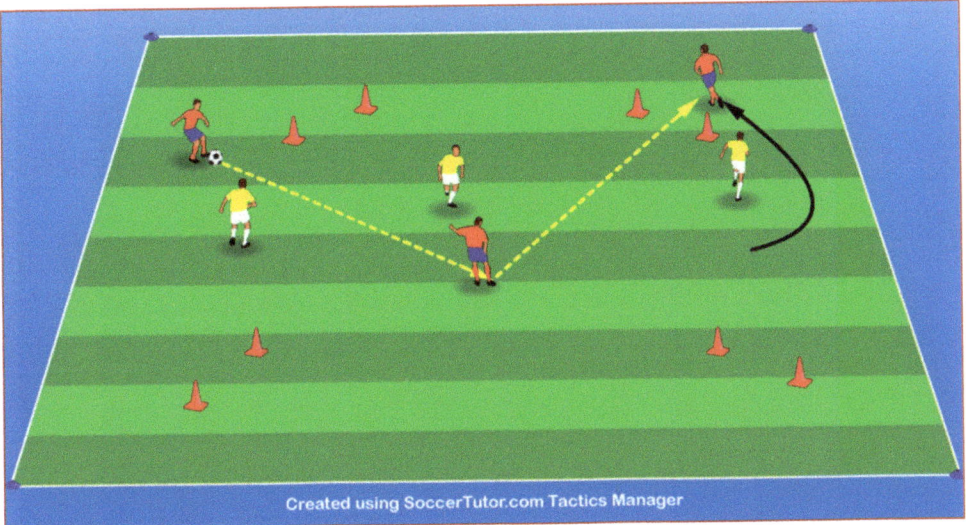

Objective
We work on creating space, player movement and accurate passing.

Description
Use a large area for the age/level of the players and play a 3v3 game. Mark out 4 cone gates.

A goal is scored when the ball is passed between the cones to a teammate who is able receive and get the ball under good control.

This is a demanding game that should not exceed 2 minutes without having a break. The players have unlimited touches.

Coaching Points
1. There should always be one goal more than the number of teams so that a team is unable to simply block the goals.
2. Play with a high tempo to create opportunities to pass through the gates.
3. Create space and lose the marker to fully exploit the large amount of space.
4. The pass in between the cones needs to be well timed and weighted to the run.

Fernando Gaspar China National Team Coach

Acceleration and Explosive Power with Physical Resistance

8 min

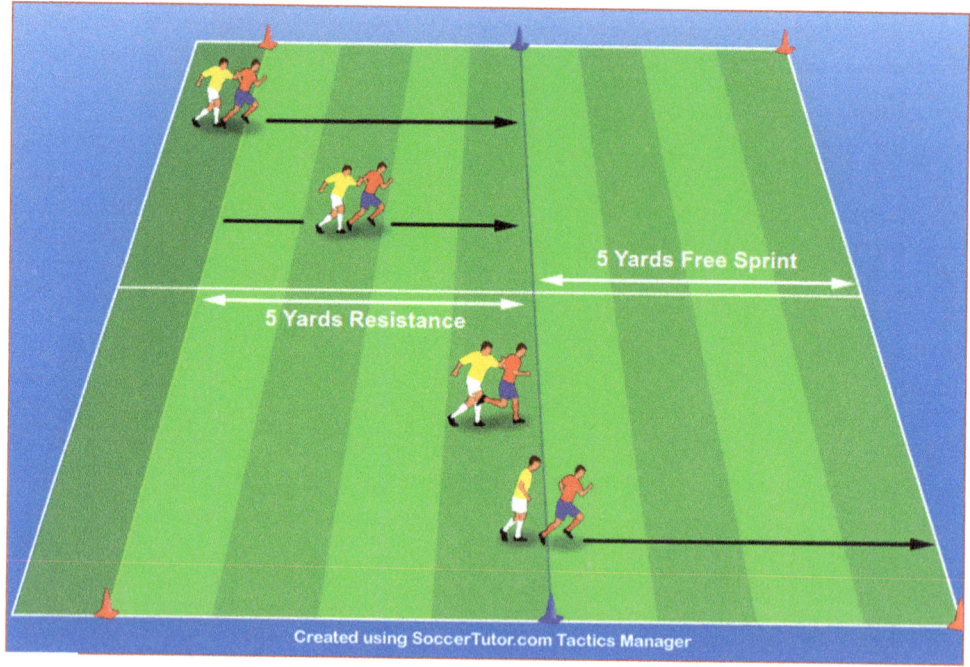

Objective
To develop explosive power by sprinting with physical resistance.

Description
Players are in pairs and the red cones are 10 yards apart. One player sets off running with his teammate providing resistance (depending on the strength of the runner) for 5 yards and then runs at full speed without resistance for the other 5 yards.

Repeat 10 times, 5 times each. Change the roles every time so that no player takes 2 consecutive turns.

Coaching Point
Monitor the level of resistance, paying special sttention to the age/level of the players.

Fernando Gaspar China National Team Coach

Ball Control and Dribbling Exercise in Channels 8 min

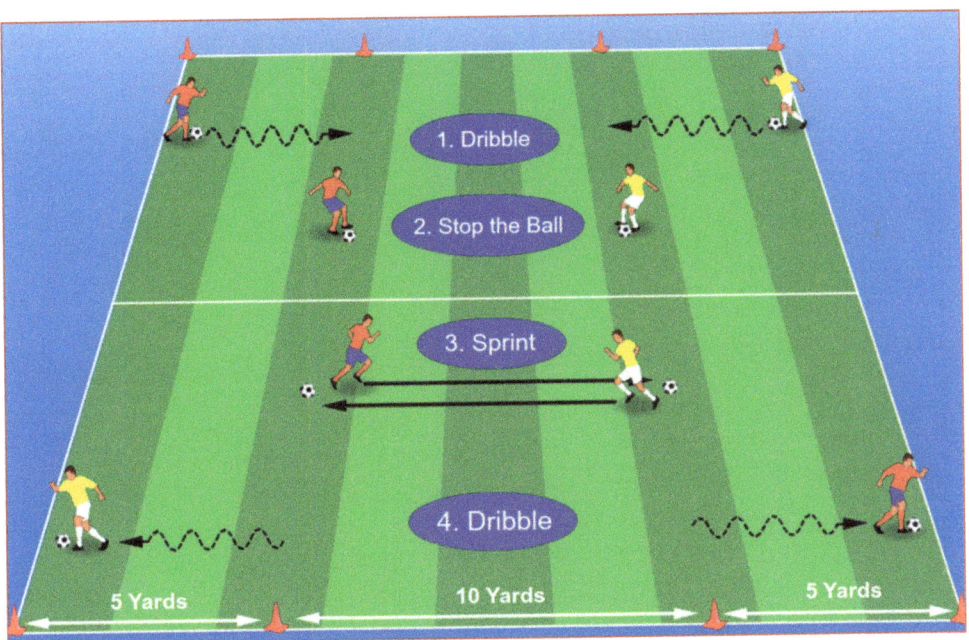

Objective
To develop control and speed on and off the ball.

Description
We mark out 4 cones with the first pair 5 yards apart, the middle ones 10 yards apart and the last pair 5 yards apart again. 2 players set off at the same time dribbling towards each other until they reach the second cone, where they stop the ball dead and leave it there.

Both players then run 10 yards to the next cone (accelerating) where they collect the ball that their teammate has left and dribble for 5 yards to the last cone.

Perform 3 series of 3 repetitions with a 45 second rest between each series.

Coaching Point
Players need to use soft touches throughout to keep the ball close to their feet.

Fernando Gaspar China National Team Coach

Running with the Ball and Changing Speed

8 min

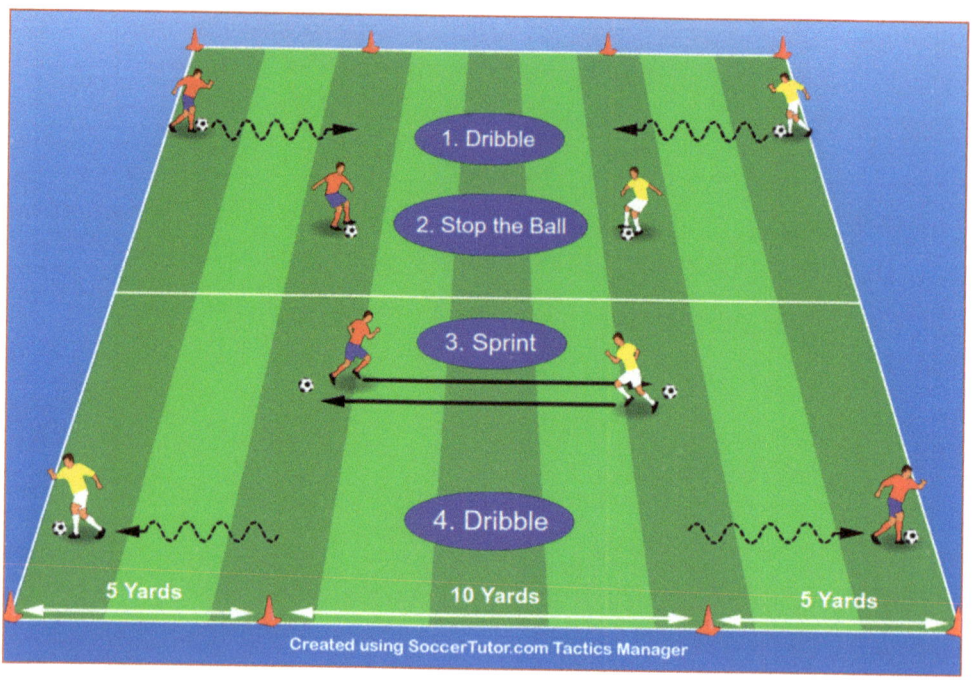

Objective
To develop complete control of the football when changing pace - stop, start, slow, fast.

Description
We have exactly the same area and layout as the previous practice, but now the focus is on changing the pace when dribbling.

The first 5 yards should be done at a high pace before the players stop the ball dead. They then dribble 10 yards at a slow pace before speeding up again for the final 5 yards.

Perform 3 series of 3 repetitions with a 45 second rest between each series.

Coaching Point
The players should practice dribbling, stopping and starting with all parts of their feet to maximise control.

Fernando Gaspar China National Team Coach

Agility and Support Play in a One Touch Passing Combination Practice

8 min

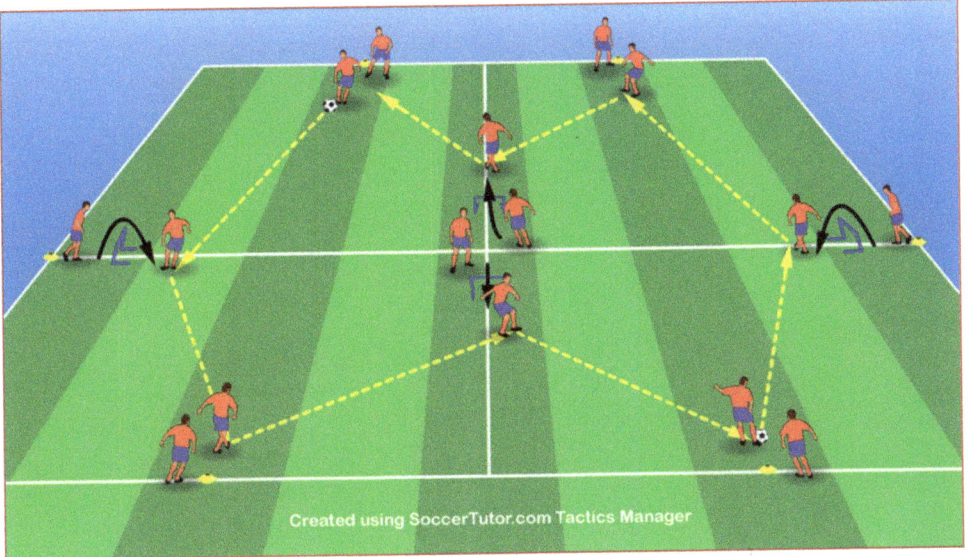

Objective
To develop passing and receiving, correct body shape and explosive jumping power.

Description
Play in an area suitable for the age/level of the players. We start with 2 balls diagonally opposite to each other as shown in the diagram.

The passes follow the sequence shown and there is a hurdle in some positions which must be jumped before the player controls the ball (receives) and then passes it to the next position.

There should be 2-3 players in each position and we always use 2 balls at a time.

Coaching Points
1. Move to meet the ball and approach it half-turned in the central positions.
2. The correct body shape should be monitored (opening up) and receiving the ball with the back foot (foot furthest away from the ball).
3. Change the direction of the drill so that the players pass and receive with both feet.
4. You can replace hurdles with speed rings or ladders to work on coordination.

Fernando Gaspar China National Team Coach

Changing Direction at Speed and Shooting Practice

8 min

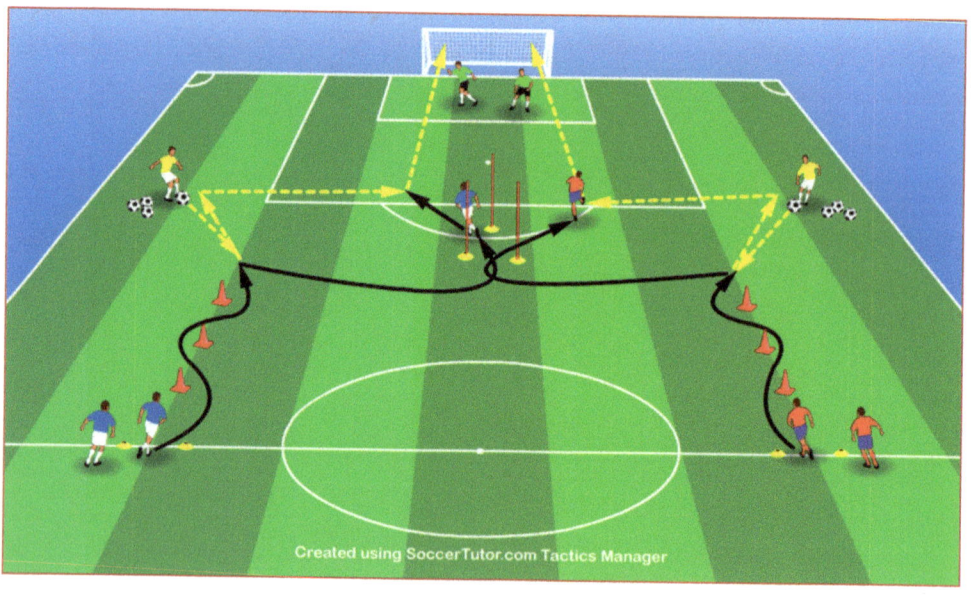

Objective
To develop quick changes of direction, combination play and shooting from the edge of the penalty area.

Description
Using half a full sized pitch, we have 2 lines of players. They slalom through the cones before playing a 1-2 combination with a teammate or coach (yellow).

They then sprint towards the centre and around the pole to receive the next pass and shoot from the edge of the box.

Both players should shoot at the same time, so if it is possible, put 2 goalkeepers in the goal.

Coaching Points
1. The final pass and run around the pole needs to be well timed and coordinated.
2. When receiving the final pass, the first touch needs to push the ball away from the body allowing space to strike through the middle of the ball with their head over it.
3. If possible, players should try to shoot first time.

Fernando Gaspar China National Team Coach

Power and Speed in a 3 v 3 Small Sided Game

10 min

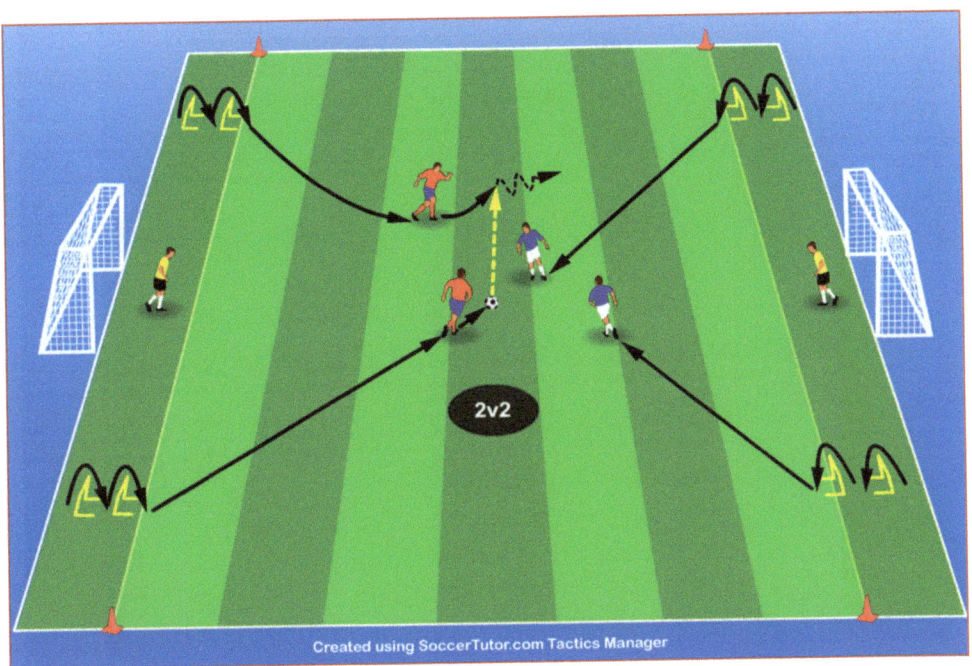

Objective
To develop agility, explosive power and speed within a small sided game.

Description
In an area 30 x 30 yards, the 4 outfield players start in the 4 corners and we have 2 goalkeepers in the goals.

Before entering the main zone, the 4 outfield players must jump over 2 hurdles. They then race to the ball in the centre and we play a normal 3v3 small sided game.

The game should last 2 minutes. The players have a break as they walk back to the corners.

Coaching Points
1. The players should look to keep their feet together and get good height when they are jumping the hurdles to work on their explosive power.
2. Encourage the players to use feints/moves to beat in 1v1 duels to attack the space in behind their opponent.

Fernando Gaspar China National Team Coach

Agility, Speed, Strength and Fast 3 v 3 Attack in a Continuous Circuit

10 min

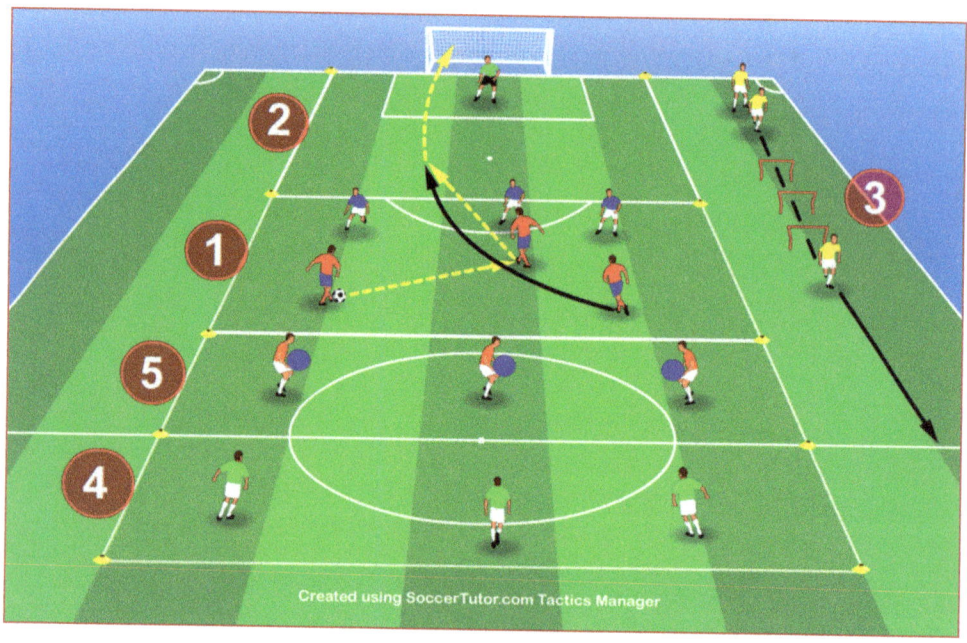

Objective
We work on agility, speed, strength, attacking and defending in a continuous circuit.

Description
Using more than half a full sized pitch, we mark out zones as shown in the diagram. We divide the players into groups of 3 and we have 5 different tasks which take 15 seconds each:

Group 1 - The 3 players use attacking combinations to score inside the penalty area.
Group 2 - The 3 players defend the attack and try to win the ball.
Group 3 - The 3 players sprint, jump the 3 hurdles and then sprint to halfway line.
Group 4 - The 3 players have 15 seconds recuperation time.
Group 5 - The 3 players perform strength exercises with medicine balls.

Coaching Points
1. Determine the exact strength exercise yourself if you do not have medicine balls.
2. For the attack, players should make runs into the space behind the defenders.

Fernando Gaspar China National Team Coach

Changing Pace and Direction with Quick Feet in a Speed Exercise with One-Two Combination

10 min

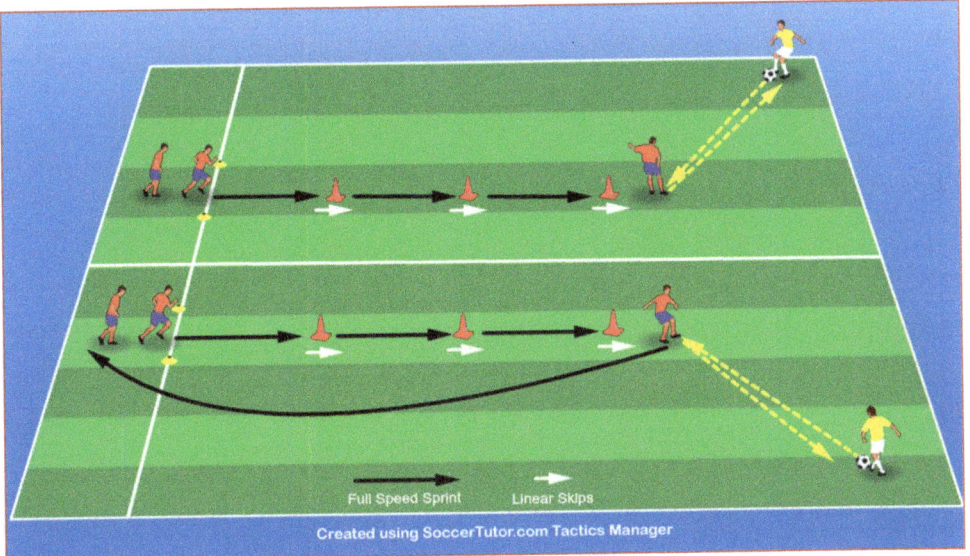

Objective
To develop speed, acceleration, deceleration, coordination and quick feet.

Description
We split the players into 2 groups and they line up facing 3 cones, each 5 yards apart.

The players set off at full speed and decelerate at the first cone. In between the next 2 cones, they sprint at full speed again, decelerate and perform linear skips past the cones (as shown in the diagram).

At the last cone they play a 1-2 combination with a teammate (yellow) and then run back to the starting position. Make sure to have a 30 second break every 2.5 minutes.

Coaching Points
1. To decelerate the players need to shorten their steps and bend their knees.
2. The intensity and speed of the exercise needs to be high throughout.

Fernando Gaspar China National Team Coach

Support Angles in a 4 v 1 Possession Exercise

15 min

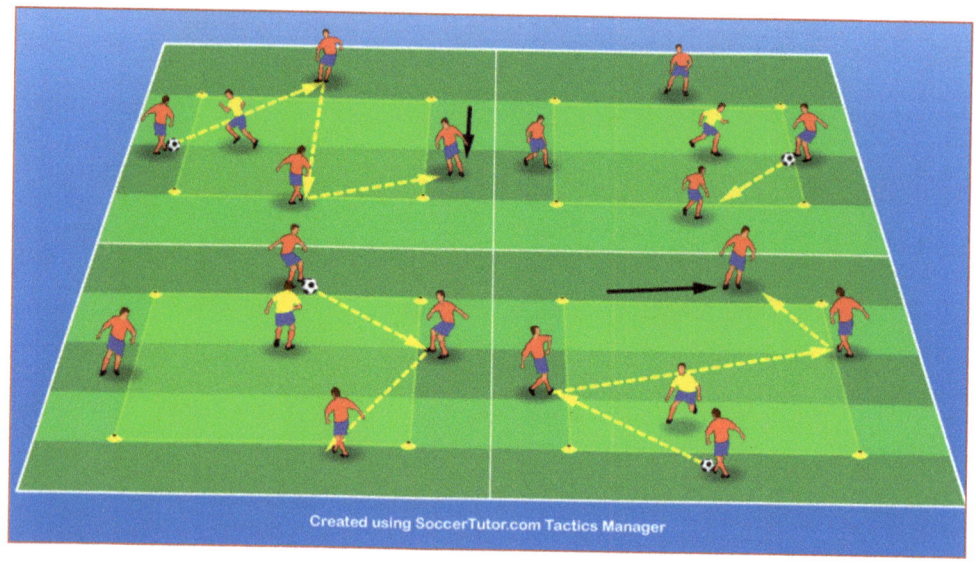

Objective
To develop all the necessary technical aspects for keeping possession under high intensity.

Description
In an area of 6 x 6 yards, we split into 4 groups. We have 4 players with possession outside the square and 1 defender inside. Players are limited to 1 touch.

The player in the middle must prevent the 4 players from completing 10 passes. If the defender wins the ball, the player who lost it then moves into the middle to defend.

If a player has been in the middle for too long without winning the ball, change the roles.

Coaching Points
1. The correct support angles should be monitored throughout so that every player has at least 2 easy passing options.
2. Players should let the ball run across their body to enable sufficient time for movement and to open up the options available.
3. Pass with the back foot whenever possible (foot furthest away from the ball).

Strength & Conditioning Circuit Games

Fernando Gaspar China National Team Coach

Technical, Speed and Conditioning Training in a Continuous Circuit

15 min

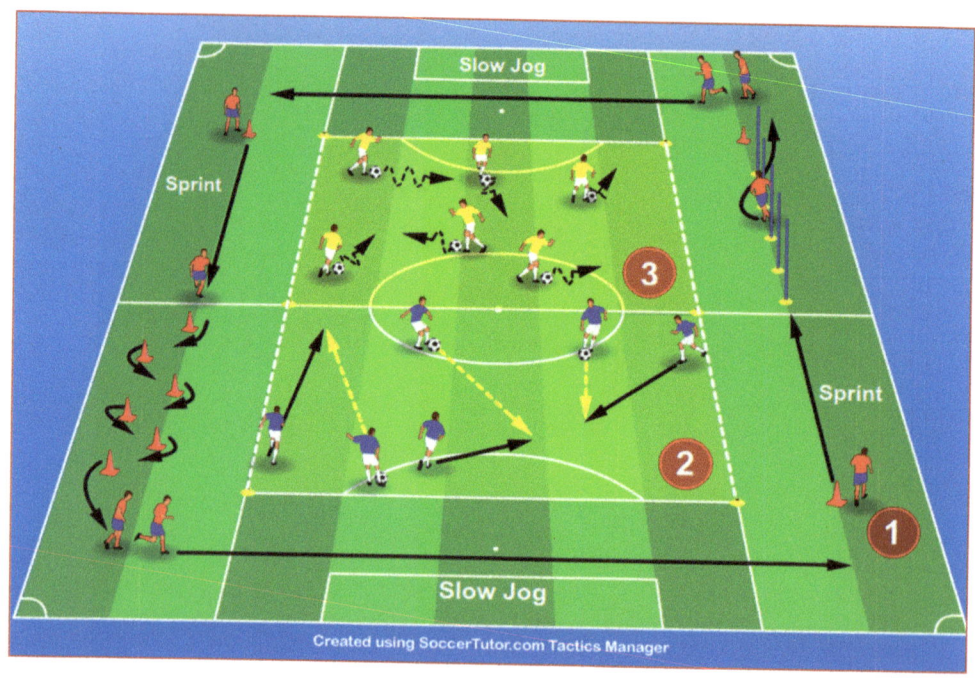

Objective
We work on acceleration, speed, passing, movement and ball control in a conditioning circuit.

Description
Using a full sized pitch, we have 3 groups of 6-8 players. We mark out 3 separate zones (A, B and C). Change the players' zone every 5 minutes.

In Zone A, 4 pairs of players (red) work at a varied pace (forwards, backwards, sideways) starting from the 4 corners of the full pitch. *Intensity: Heart rate 140-160 bpm (maintain a regular rhythm).*

In Zone B, pairs of players (blue) pass the ball (2-3 touches) and play the ball into empty areas for their partner to run onto. In Zone C, each player (yellow) runs with a ball, practicing different types of dribbling, turns or feints.

Fernando Gaspar China National Team Coach

Conditioning Exercise With and Without the Ball: One-Two Combination Running Circuit

15 min

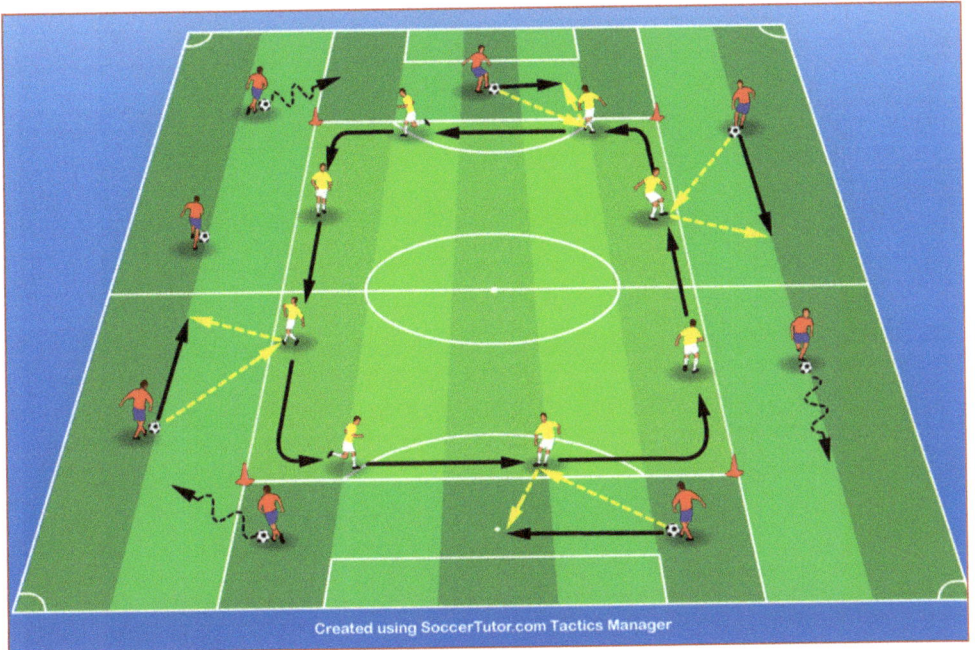

Objective
We work on acceleration, deceleration and one-two combinations.

Description
We work with the same area as the previous practice, but this time we work on acceleration and deceleration. There are 8 players on the outside who have a ball each and 8 players on the inside.

The short distance on the outside should be taken at speed, with ball control over the longer distances.

The red players run with the ball and the yellow players run at a moderate pace. The blue players run with the ball in one direction and play a 1-2 with the yellow players running in the opposite direction. After 1.5 minutes change the direction.

Change the roles every 3 minutes with a 1 minute break in between each series. *Intensity: Heart rate 130-150 / 140-160 bpm.*

Fernando Gaspar China National Team Coach

Tactical Shape with Position Specific Passing and Conditioning Exercise

25-30 min

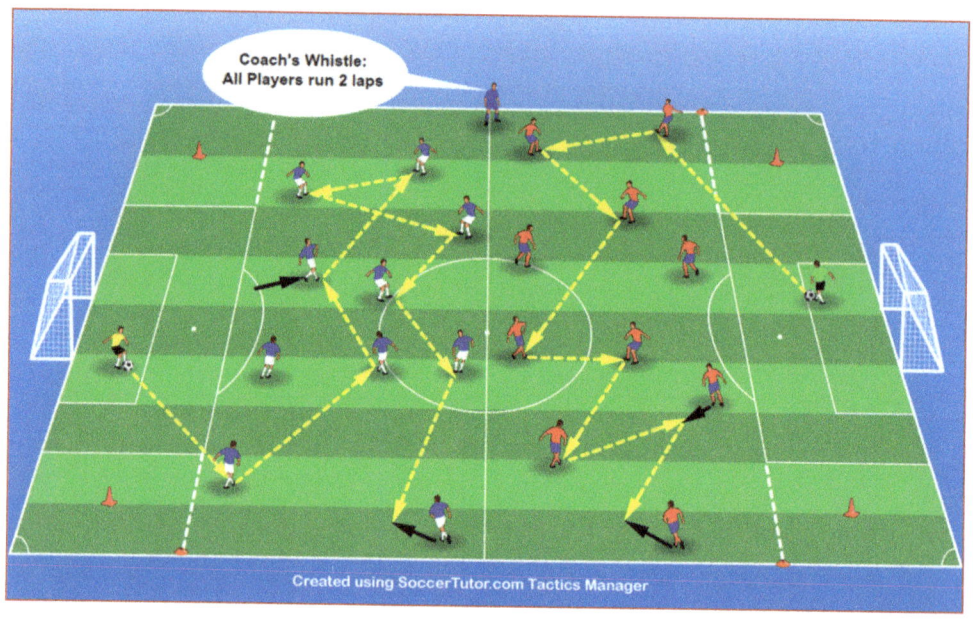

Objective
To develop tactical movements and passing in the possession phase with lap running.

Description
Using a full sized pitch, we have 2 teams of 11 (or 10) players in each half. Use the players in the positions they are in during competitive games.

The ball starts with the goalkeeper and each team must keep the ball with a maximum of 3 touches per player. All of the players are constantly moving, maintaining a tight formation and switching the play.

After 3 minutes and on the coach's whistle, all of the players must do 2 laps around the pitch, starting from one of the cones. Then continue with the same exercise.

Change the player's positions. The coach directs the exercise and dictates the pace. Perform 2 x series of 12-15 minutes. *Intensity: Heart rate 160-170 / 175 bpm.*

Fernando Gaspar China National Team Coach

Conditioning Circuit: 6 v 6 Practice Game and Interval Training

15-30 min

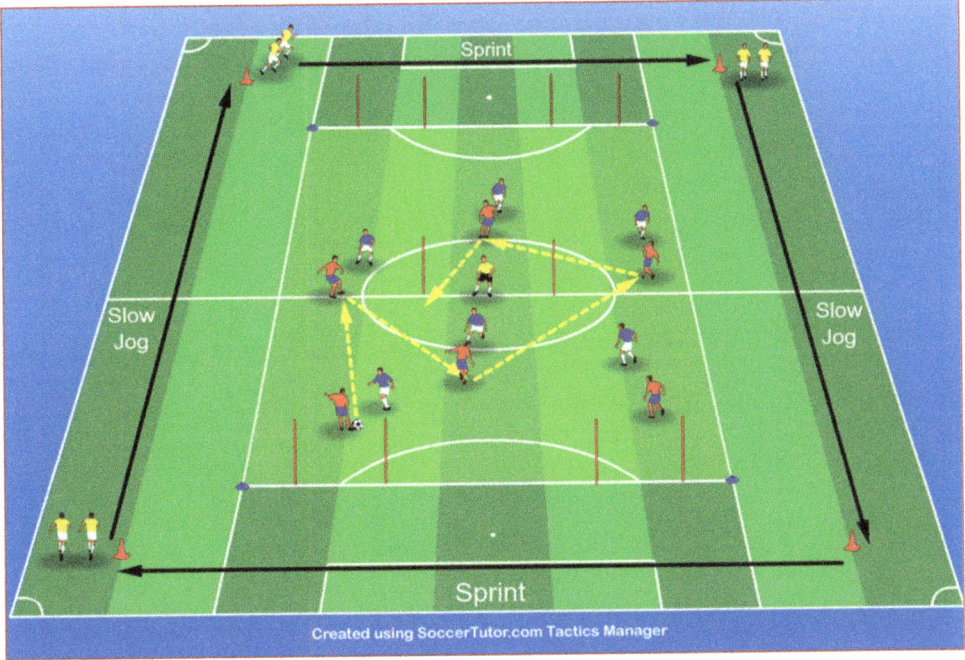

Objective
To develop conditioning levels using interval training and a small sided game.

Description
Using a full sized pitch, we have 3 teams of 6 players and a neutral goalkeeper.

In the central zone, there are 4 small goals (2 yards wide) and 1 large goal. 2 teams (red and blue) play a 6v6 small sided game with unlimited touches. The teams try to score in the opposition's small goals or either side of the large goal. A goal can be scored by either shooting or running the ball through the goal.

During the game, the third team run around the field of play at a varied place (diagram example = sprint the width of the pitch, slow jog for the length).

After 5 minutes, change the teams around. *Intensity: Heart rate 160-180 bpm.*

Fernando Gaspar China National Team Coach

Technical Passing, Combination Play and Conditioning Practice

15 min

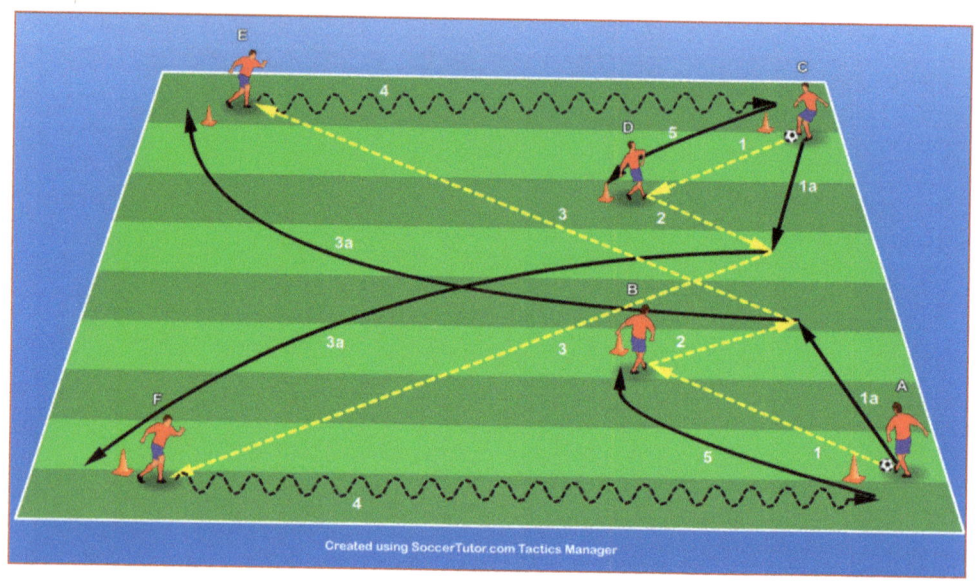

Objective
To develop the correct speed, weight and timing of the passing (both along the ground and in the air) and the timing/angle of the movement, as well as working on conditioning.

Description
In an area 20 x 20 yards we have a technical interval training resistance circuit and work with 6 players. We start simultaneously with players A and C who both have a ball. Player A plays a short pass to B and C plays a short pass to D. Player B returns the ball (first touch) for A to run onto and Player D does the same for C.

Player A passes the ball diagonally to E and follows the ball with a curved run. Player C passes to F and does the same. Players E and F control the ball and dribble it towards the starting positions which are now occupied by Players B and D. They then move to the next position to receive the first pass as the sequence is repeated.

Repeat 3-5 series and rest for 1-2 minutes between each series. *Intensity: Heart rate 160-170 / 180 bpm.*

Fernando Gaspar China National Team Coach

Agility, Coordination and Speed Interval Training   15-20 min

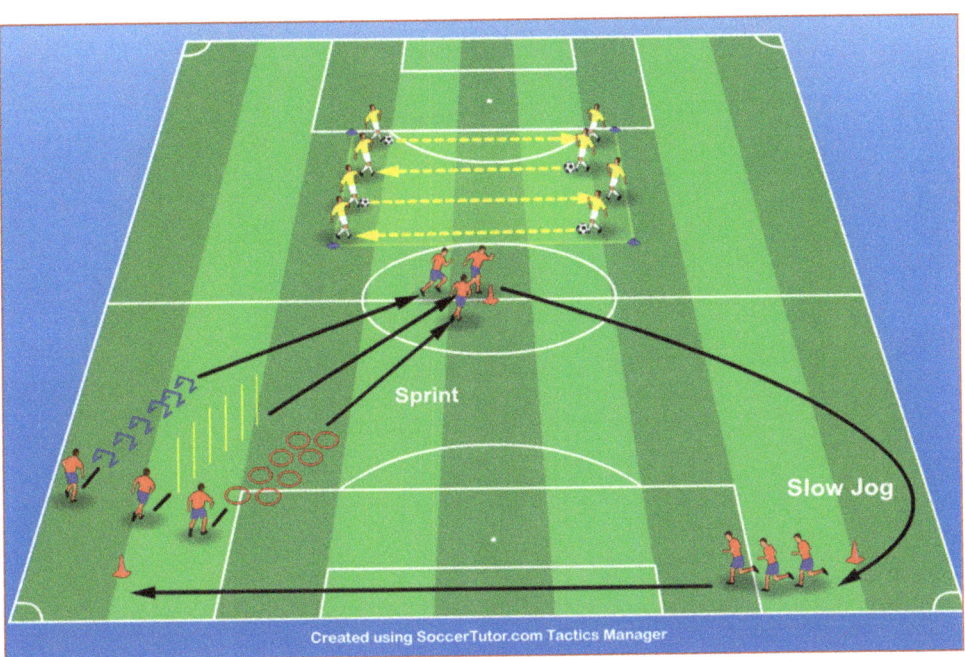

Objective
In this conditioning exercise we also work on agility, speed, acceleration and coordination.

Description
We use a full sized pitch and have 2 groups of 8-9 players. The reds work in groups of 3, starting at one of the 3 cones and perform 3 series of the whole circuit without rest.

At the first cone the players either perform 6 explosive standing jumps over the hurdles with their feet together, slalom through the poles at a high speed or perform 8 explosive lateral jumps (alternating legs).

This is followed by 10 seconds intense sprinting for 35-50 yards to the second cone. At the second cone, the players jog slowly round the third cone and to the start (30 seconds slow jogging - 100 yards total). *Intensity: Heart rate 160- 180 bpm.*

The yellow group perform technical passes in pairs varying from 1-2 touches. Swap the roles of the groups after the reds complete their 3 series of the circuit.

Fernando Gaspar China National Team Coach

Interval Training with Technical Work in a 5 Zone Circuit

15-20 min

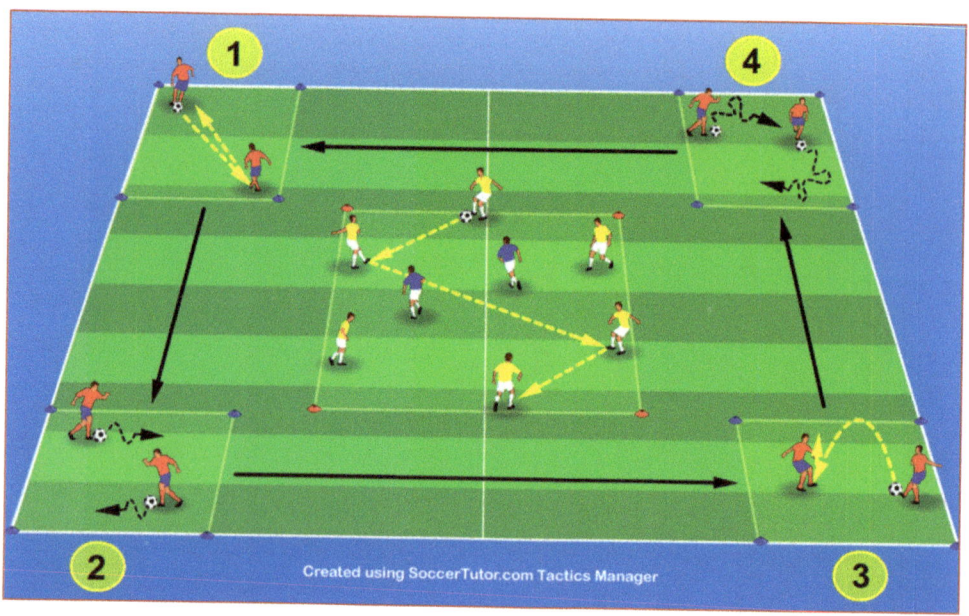

Objective
To work on conditioning with a focus on short sprints and developing technical actions.

Description
Here we work with 2 groups of 8 players. The corner zones are 5 x 5 yards and the central zone is 10 x 10 yards. The red players work in pairs in each technical zone and the yellow players play a 6v2 possession game.

The red players perform their technical actions at a moderate pace for 20-30 seconds (insist on technical quality). In Zone 1 they pass with the left/right foot, Zone 2 is individual touches (ball control), Zone 3 is ball juggling in a pair and Zone 4 is dribbling with dummies/feints.

The red pairs then sprint to the next zone (5 -10 seconds). A series is complete once they have performed all 4 technical actions and 4 sprints. Perform 3 series with 1 minute of rest time in between each series. *Intensity: Heart rate 160-180 bpm.*

Once 3 series have been completed, the reds swap with the players in the central zone and play a 6v2 game while they recuperate. Change the 2 defenders often.

Fernando Gaspar China National Team Coach

Conditioning with Position Specific Team Shape Exercise

25 min

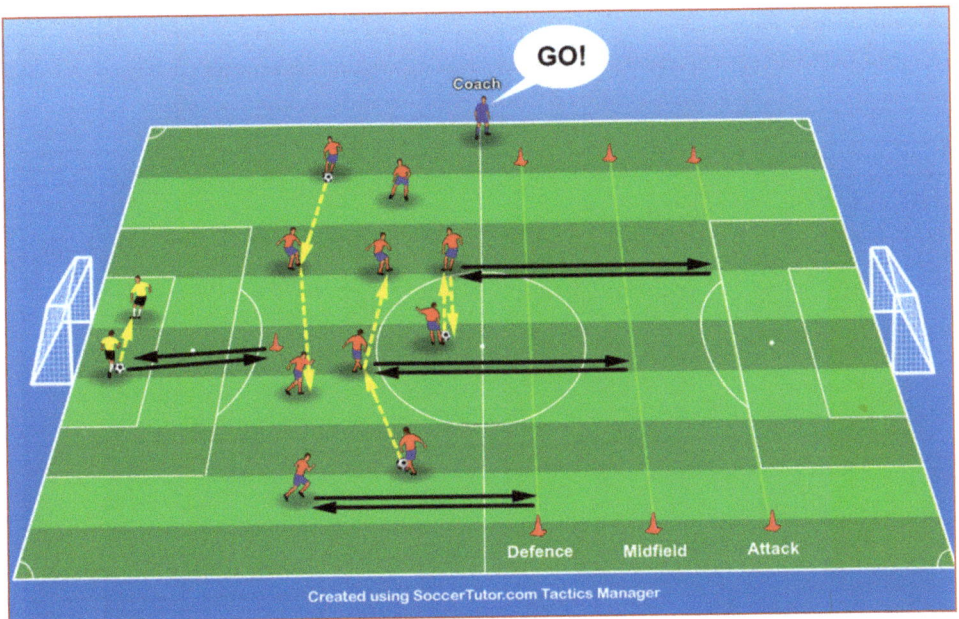

Objective
To develop conditioning levels while also working on tactical shape/passing.

Description
Using a full sized pitch, the players take up their usual playing positions in one half (4-4-2 example in diagram). We place cones in the other half of the pitch for the defence, midfield and attacking lines. There is also a cone outside the area for the goalkeepers.

The players play the ball between themselves along their positional lines at a moderate pace. On the coach's signal, the players must run at 80% of their maximum speed to the correct line in the opposite side of the pitch and back again. They then continue to pass the ball as before. Vary the skills or technical movements.

After the 15 second run (70-75 yards) the players rest for 20-30 seconds. Repeat this 3 times. Perform the whole series twice with 2 minutes rest between each series.

Intensity: Heart rate 160-180/185 bpm.

Fernando Gaspar China National Team Coach

Endurance 8 v 8 Small Sided Game with Dribbling End Zones + Sprinting Exercise

25-30 min

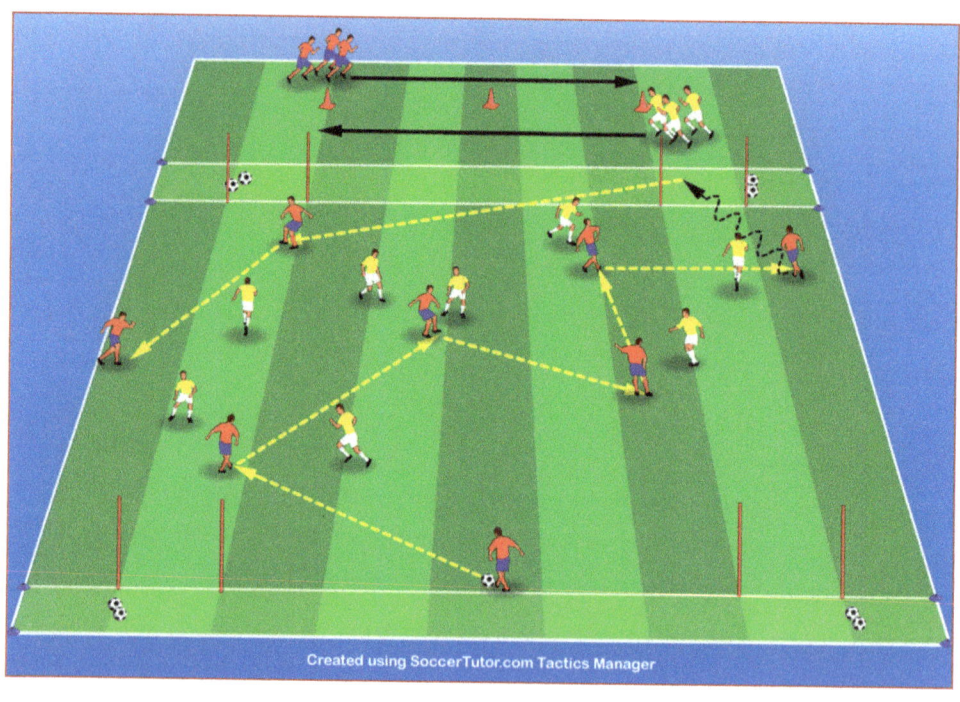

Objective
To develop speed, acceleration and conditioning/endurance.

Description
In an area 40 x 25 yards, 2 teams of 8 (or 9) players play a small sided game. Behind the game area, we have 3 cones 15 yards apart.

The small sided game is played with unlimited touches and a goal is scored when a player dribbles through the poles in the opposition half. The team that scores retains possession.

Halfway through the game (approximately 5 minutes), the players on both teams must perform 3 to 5 progressive accelerations (from 70% to 100% of maximum speed) over 30 yards, with 30 seconds rest between each one. When finished, perform another 3 to 5 progressive accelerations (repeat) before finishing the second half of the game.

Intensity: Heart rate 150-175 bpm. Active recuperation: Return heart rate to 120 bpm.

Fernando Gaspar China National Team Coach

Goalkeeper Support Play and Conditioning in a 3 Zone Continuous Possession Game

20-25 min

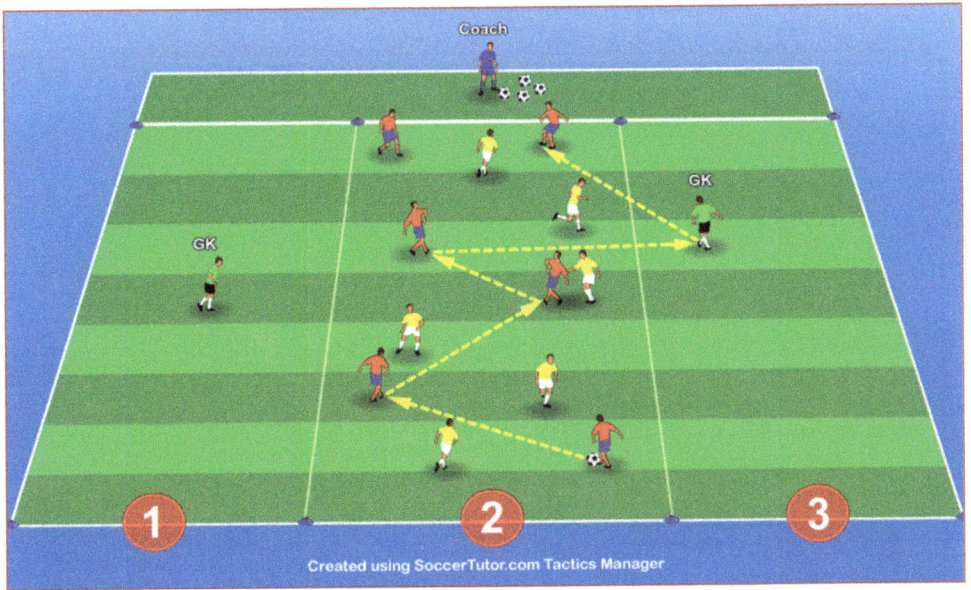

Objective
To work on the technical actions needed to maintain possession while developing the players' levels of conditioning.

Description
In an area 25 x 20 yards, divide the pitch into 3 numbered zones. We play with 2 teams of 6 players and 2 neutral goalkeepers who can only use their feet.

The aim is to keep possession and pass the ball around the zones. You can play with unlimited touches or limit the players to 2 or 3 touches. The game can take place in 1, 2 or 3 zones, depending on the coach's instructions.

The goalkeepers stay behind the zone as support. If the ball goes out, the coach immediately passes in another. Count the number of consecutive passes a team achieves.

Play 3 series of 5 minutes with 2 minutes rest in between each series. *Intensity: Heart rate 160-180 bpm.*

Fernando Gaspar China National Team Coach

Explosive Power 6 v 6 Fast Support Play Dynamic Small Sided Game

30-35 min

All players need to move into attacking half before goal can be scored

Objective
To develop conditioning levels within a continuous technical small sided game.

Description
In an area 50 x 40 yards, we work with 3 teams of 5 players + 2 goalkeepers and play a small sided game. If the ball goes out, the coach immediately passes another in (continuous).

Limit the number of touches in the defensive zone (defenders) and allow unlimited touches in the attacking zone (attackers). A goal only counts when all of the players on the attacking team have crossed the middle line. If one of the opposition players is still in the other half when a team scores, the goal counts double.

The games last 6 minutes with a 2 minute rest afterwards. Change the teams round every 2 minutes so each team plays 4 minutes and has 2 minutes recuperation on the sidelines. Play a total of 4 games. *Intensity: Heart rate 165- 180 bpm.*

Fernando Gaspar China National Team Coach

Aerobic Power 8 v 8 Small Sided Game   20 min

Objective
To develop conditioning levels within a continuous technical small sided game.

Description
In an area 50 x 40 yards, we work with 2 teams of 8 players + 2 goalkeepers. We have a 4v4 situation inside with each team having an extra 4 players outside in the positions shown.

We play a small sided game with both teams trying to score using their outside players.

When the ball goes out of play, the goalkeeper of the team in possession must quickly restart the game. The inside players have unlimited touches. The outside players and goalkeepers are limited to 1 touch.

Play 4 x 4 minute games with 1 minute rest in between each game. The coach swaps the player roles after every game. *Intensity: Heart rate 170- 190 bpm.*

Football Coaching Specialists Since 2001

Tactics Manager Software

Get Easy to use Soccer Coaching Software to Create your own Professional Looking Training Drills, Tactics, Formations and Sessions

To Buy your Copy, Visit:

www.SoccerTutor.com/TacticsManager

visit   www.soccertutor.com   contact info@soccertutor.com   tel +44 (0)208 1234 007

Football Coaching Specialists Since 2001

120 Practices from the Coaches of Real Madrid, Atlético Madrid & Athletic Bilbao

To Buy your Copy, Visit:
www.SoccerTutor.com

visit www.soccertutor.com   contact info@soccertutor.com   tel +44 (0)208 1234 007

www.ingramcontent.com/pod-product-compliance
Lightning Source LLC
Chambersburg PA
CBHW041732300426
44116CB00018B/2956